The Professional Programmers Guide to

C

Pat McKay
Department of Business Administration
Glasgow College

Pitman

PITMAN PUBLISHING
128 Long Acre, London WC2E 9AN

First published in Great Britain 1989

British Library Cataloguing in Publication Data
McKay, Pat
The professional programmers guide to C.—
(The professional programmers guides).
1. Computer systems. Programming languages :
C language
I. Title II. Series
005.13′3

ISBN 0 273 02958 4

Printed and bound in Great Britain at
The Bath Press, Avon

Contents

Preface

This Guide is intended as an introduction to the basic fundamentals of the C programming language. It is suitable for both first time programmers and as an introduction to the C language for experienced programmers.

The approach taken in this book is to take a simple problem and expand it until it reaches the stage of being a menu-driven file processing application. Throughout the text emphasis is placed on producing well- structured programs.

1 Introduction to Programming in C

The C programming language was developed during the 1970s at the Bell Laboratories, USA, for use with the UNIX operating system (later versions of UNIX are written in C). The accepted standard definition for the C programming language can be found in *The C Programming Language* by Kernighan and Ritchie (Prentice-Hall). Most C compilers conform to this standard.

C is a general purpose programming language which can neither be classed as a high level language nor as a low level language. It has all the features expected of a high level language. On the other hand it allows the programmer to access the computer's hardware and has the high performance usually expected with low level languages. Probably the best way to classify C is to consider it as a programmer's language with performance and computer access facilities found in assembler languages.

Using C it is possible to construct concise, well structured and well documented programs. On the other hand, the same program can be badly written and difficult to understand. In this book we are aiming for well written, structured and documented programs.

1.1 Example Problem - TV Rental Bills

Throughout this book the programming features of C will be introduced using the following problem and extensions to it.

A television rental company is computerising its billing system for **colour** television rentals.

The program is to input a **customer number** and the **number of weeks rent due**, calculate and output the appropriate bill.

The solution to this problem is:

input customer number and number of weeks rent due
determine rent per week for colour TV
calculate bill
print bill

TV Rental Program written in C

The TV Rental Program written in the C programming language can be seen below:

```
#include <stdio.h>

/* TV RENTAL BILLS - Version 1 - Colour TV only */

main()
{
    int no_of_weeks, customer_no;
    float rent_per_week;

    /*Input customer number and number of weeks rent due*/
    printf("\nEnter customer number ");
    scanf("%4d",&customer_no);
    printf("Enter number of weeks rent due ");
    scanf("%2d",&no_of_weeks);

    /*Determine rent per week - colour TV is 3.60*/
    rent_per_week = 3.60;

    /*Calculate bill*/
    bill = no_of_weeks * rent_per_week;

    /* Print the bill*/
    printf("\n\nTV RENTAL BILL");
    printf("\n\nCustomer number is %d", customer_no);
    printf("\nNumber of weeks rent due is %d", no_of_weeks);
    printf("\nRent per week is %.2f", rent_per_week);
    printf("\n\nRental due is %.2f\n\n", bill);
}
```

Running this program will give: (NB User responses are **in bold**)

Enter customer number **3456**
Enter number of weeks rent due **4**

TV RENTAL BILL

Customer number is 3456
Number of weeks rent due is 4

```
Rent per week is 3.60
Rental due is 14.40
```

1.2 Producing Programs in C

Computerising a problem is more than just writing it in an appropriate programming language and running it on a computer. A number of steps are involved:

1. Produce a program design for the problem
2. Construct the program using instructions from an appropriate programming language
3. Store the program in a file on a disk
4. Compile the program
5. Link the compiled program elements
6. Run the program
7. Test the program using suitable test data.
   Make corrections by repeating steps 2 to 7.

Steps 1 and 7 are covered in the next chapter.

Step 2 is covered throughout this book using the C programming language.

Steps 3 to 6 are secific to the particular C environment and compiler that is being used. However any environment must contain

- an editor to allow program commands to be entered and saved into a file.
- a compiler and associated linker.

See your manual for details of how to invoke your particular version of C and how to enter, compile, link and run your programs.

1.3 Programming Exercises

1. Enter the TV Rental Program into a file called TV1. Compile and run the program.

1.4 Introduction to the C Programming Language

The C programming language will be explored using examples from the TV Rental Program. This program contains comments, declarations, assignment statements and input/output statements.

Comments

Comments are enclosed between /* and */. They are used to document the program by explaining what the program instructions are intended to do.
e.g.

```
/* TV RENTAL BILLS - Version 1 - Colour TV only */

/*Determine rent per week - colour TV is 3.60*/
```

Declarations

Declarations are used to associate a variable name with an area of storage and to indicate the type of information that is to be stored in it. The general syntax of a declaration is

```
<data type> <list of variable names separated by commas>;
```

e.g.

```
int no_of_weeks, customer_no;
```

this declaration indicates that two variables, **no_of_weeks** and **customer_no**, are of type **integer** (i.e. whole numbers).
e.g.

```
float rent_per_week;
```

this declares one variable **rent_per_week** as a **floating point number (i.e. a number containing a decimal point).**

Data types

Data types **int** and **float** are only two of a variety of data types allowed in C. A complete list of data types is given in the following table:

Data type	*Storage space(bits)*	*Range*
int	16	-32768 to 32767
short int	8	-128 to 127
long int	32	-4294967296 to 4294967295
unsigned int	16	0 to 65535
float	32	10^{-37} to 10^{38} (to 6 significant digits)
double	64	10^{-37} to 10^{38} (to 12 significant digits)
char	8	0 to 255 (a character's ASCII value)

Variable names

Variable names should be meaningful and constructed such that they

- contain one or more characters (letters, numbers or underscore)
- must begin with a letter
- must not be the same as a C keyword
- must not have the same name as a function.

Declarations for the TV Rental Program

The problem requires two values to be input into the program (i.e. customer number and the number of weeks rent due). On input these values have to be stored somewhere in the computer, hence storage space has to be declared for them. In order to do this a variable name has to be given to each input (e.g. **customer_no** and **no_of_weeks**). As both the inputs will be whole numbers the data will be of type **int**.

The program requires one other storage space in order to hold the weekly rental. Hence a variable name must be declared for this storage area (e.g. **rent_per_week**). As the weekly rental is a monetary value it will contain a decimal point, hence it is of data type **float**.

Therefore the declarations are:

```
int no_of_weeks, customer_no;
float rent_per_week;
```

Note that all program statements in C end with a semi-colon (;).

Assignment statements

Assignment statements allow us to assign values to variables. The general syntax of an assignment statement is

<variable_name> = <expression>

e.g.

```
rent_per_week = 3.60;
```

Note that in any assignment statement

- only one variable can appear on the left hand side of the = sign
- mixed variable types may be used but the final outcome is stored in the format of the left hand variable. e.g

  ```
  float sum;
  sum = 3 + 2.5;
  ```

  gives sum a value of 5.5, but

  ```
  int sum;
  sum = 3 + 2.5;
  ```

  gives sum a value of 5.
- the right hand expression is evaluated from left to right with the arithmetic operators having the following precedence:

  %(modulo division)
  / *
  \+ -
  (NB % gives the remainder after an integer division).
- the right hand expression can contain any number of ( ) s, but there must be a closing bracket) for every opening bracket (.

Input and output

Input and output statements are not contained within the C compiler and therefore are undefined. Most C environments include input and output functions in a library. While these functions may have standard names, their implementations may be very different. Therefore, whenever a new C compiler is used the input/output functions should be carefully checked for their compatibility.

The library that contains the input and output functions is usually called

```
stdio.h
```

There has to be a statement at the beginning of all C programs which use the input and output functions to include this library. Hence at the start of the TV Rental Program is the statement

```
#include <stdio.h>
```

Input

Most C input/output libraries contain a number of input functions. However at this stage we are only concerned with the function **scanf()**. In the TV Rental Program we use scanf() twice in order to input the customer number and the number of weeks rent due:

```
scanf("%4d",&customesr_no);
scanf("%2d",&no_of_weeks);
```

The general syntax of scanf() is

```
scanf("<input_format>", <list_of_variables>)
```

where <input_format> is a list of input control arguments of the form

```
% * maximum_field_width l conversion_character
```

where

* indicates the suppression of an assignment, i.e. it allows sections of the input data to be skipped.

For example

```
scanf("%d%*d%d", &no_1, &no_2);
```

with the input data

```
26 33 47
```

will result in no_1 having the value 26, 33 will be skipped (i.e. the presence of * in the input format) and no_2 will have the value 47.

maximum_field_width is the maximum number of characters to be input and stored in a particular variable. Hence inputs can be separated by spaces, a new line character or by a specified number of characters.
For example

```
scanf("%2d %1d %3d %d", &no_1, &no_2, &no_3, &no_4);
```

with the input data

```
36726 8
```

will result in the variable no_1 having the value 36 (i.e. %2d)
no_2 7 (i.e. %1d)
no_3 26 (i.e. %3d but terminated by the space)
no_4 8 (i.e. %d)

conversion_character is used to indicate how the input field is to be interpreted. Conversion characters available are:

Conversion character	*Corresponding variable type*	*Interpretation*
d	int	decimal integer
h	short int	short integer
f	double	floating point number
o	int	octal number
x	int	hexadecimal integer
c	char	single character, does not skip spaces
s	char string	character string (will automatically store the character \0 (zero) at the end of the string)

l (letter l) may precede the conversion characters d, o and x to indicate that they are of type **long integer**.

Now consider the <list_of_variables>. Note that each variable is preceded by an &. This indicates that we are referring to the **address** (or **location**) of the variable, rather than the variable itself. In other words the variable_list is a **list of pointers** indicating where the inputs are to be put.

For example

&no_1 is a pointer to the address (location) of the variable no_1.

Pointers are discussed at length in chapter 5.

In the majority of cases the variable_list will consist of only one variable. This is in order that a prompt can be output using **printf()** to indicate the particular input required.

Output

The most common method of sending output to the screen is to use the function

```
printf("<output_format>",<list_of_variables>);
```

Consider some of the printf() statements in the TV Rental Program:

(a)

```
printf("\nEnter customer number ");
```

This gives a new line (\n) and then outputs the text

```
Enter customer number
```

(b)

```
printf("\n\nCustomer number is %d", customer_no);
```

This gives two new lines (\n\n) then outputs the text

```
Customer number is
```

followed by the value of customer number under format %d (integer). Therefore, if the customer number was 3456, the output would be

```
Customer number is 3456
```

(c)

```
printf("\n\nRental due is %.2f\n\n", bill);
```

This gives two new lines then outputs

Rental due is

followed by the value of the variable bill as a decimal number with two decimal places (%.2f). Hence if the value of bill is 14.40 the output would be

Rental due is 14.40

(d)

It is also possible to combine the five printf() statements into one.

```
printf("\n\nTV RENTAL BILL \n\nCustomer number is %d \n
    Number of weeks rent due is %d \nRent per week is %.2f
    \n\nRental due is %.2f\n\n", customer_no, rent_per_week,
    bill);
```

From the above examples it can be seen that the <output_format>, enclosed in " ", consists of three types of information:

- text
- character preceded by a \ (e.g. \n)
- characters following a % (e.g. %d, %.2f).

\ and % can appear anywhere within the quotes.

There are a number of \ codes:

\code	*Effect*
\b	backspace
\f	form feed
\n	new line
\r	carriage return
\t	horizontal tab
\'	single quote
\0 (zero)	null

The % character is used to indicate the way in which the value of a variables is to be printed. The general syntax is

%	
minus sign	indicating left justification
minimum field width	
	separator
precision	e.g. number of decimal places, maximum number of characters to be printed from string
l (letter l)	indicating that the data item is of type **long**
conversion character	data type

For example,

%6.2f

would output a decimal number with two decimal places over a field width of 6 characters (e.g. 1.5 would be output as two spaces followed by 1.50, i.e. 1.50).

The conversion characters are:

Conversion character	*Format*
d	integer
f	decimal floating point
e	decimal notation of the form ±m.nnnnnnE±xx
g	use f or e, whichever is shorter
c	single character
s	string of characters
o	unsigned octal
x	unsigned hexadecimal
u	unsigned decimal

1.5 Programming Exercises

1. Write a program that will output your name and address such that (a) it all appears on one line, and (b) it appears as it would on an envelope.

2. Write a program that will input a temperature in degrees Celsius. Using the formula

$$C = (5/9)*(F - 32)$$

the program will calculate and print the input temperature in degrees Fahrenheit.

3. Write a program that will input the length and breadth of a rectangle (measured in a whole number of feet). The program will then calculate and output the area (in square yards) and the perimeter (in yards) of the rectangle.

2 Introduction To Structured Programming

During the past few years there has been mounting concern over the increasing costs of producing computer programs. Programming costs fall into two categories

- program development
- program maintenance

A number of survey's have been carried out which show that the bulk of programming costs occur in maintaining the program rather than in developing it. One way of reducing these costs is to produce well structured programs. These are usually easier to test and therefore less errors are likely to occur during the programs life. Any alterations or corrections that have to be made are easier to make as the program code is straight forward to follow. When corrections are made to a structured program they are isolated in a small section of code rather than being in the heart of a long piece of code, avoiding programs having to be re-written from scratch. In producing a good program it should be structured in such a way that

- it is coded to **MATCH** the program design. If this is done properly, then a change to one part of the design should only require a change to one part of the program code.
- it is **SIMPLE**. The code should be both easy to follow and obvious. If complex instructions have to be used to enhance the program's efficiency, then they should be well-documented within the program. The program should be written using instructions that come readily to mind. Remember, the chances are that if you have to keep looking at the manual for appropriate instructions they will be too complex.
- any **MACHINE DEPENDENT** statements used should be well documented. These are often impossible to avoid, particularly for screen handling and graphics.
- there is only one **EXIT** route from the program.
- it should be built up from a number of subroutines and/or functions, each of which should have only one **ENTRY** point and one

EXIT point.

- it should have **MEANINGFUL** variable and subroutine/function names.
- the program code should be well laid out. **INDENTATION** should be used to indicate the start and finish of loops. It then becomes obvious when end-of-loop statements are missing.
- **SIMPLICITY** should never be sacrificed for speed. If it is too slow then its the wrong design, or is using inadequate hardware or an unsuitable implementation language.

Using structured programming techniques it is possible to produce computer programs that conform to the above requirements.

The following diagram shows the steps involved in developing a computer program using structured program techniques. Each stage of development should automatically provide supporting documentation for the final program. As far as this book is concerned the only restriction to using this method for developing our programs is that C has already been selected as the language that will be used for implementing the programs.

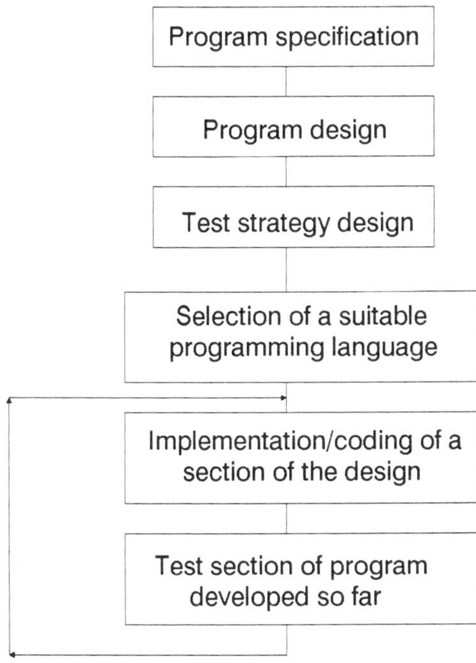

Looking closely at this diagram it should be obvious that the bulk of program development time is spent in designing the program. It is at this stage that use is made of structured programming techniques.

2.1 Structured Programming Techniques

In this book we will be using two main structured programming techniques, that of

- module relationship charts
- pseudo code

Module relationship charts

This assumes that any problem and, therefore, any associated program is made up of a number of modules. Initially module relationship charts are used to break the problem down into a number of sub-problems. Each sub-problem is represented by a module. Each module is then broken down into further modules until each module performs **one** function (that does not mean one programming instruction) which cannot be broken down any further. Therefore, module relationship charts are used to show the **relationship** between modules. Hence a module relationship chart is of the form:

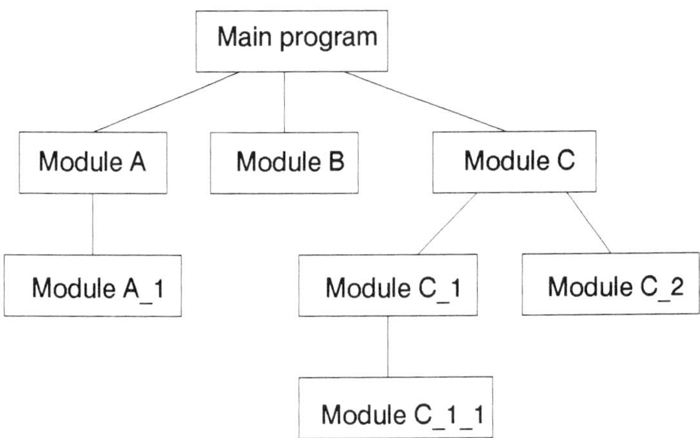

The module relationship chart for the TV Rental problem is:

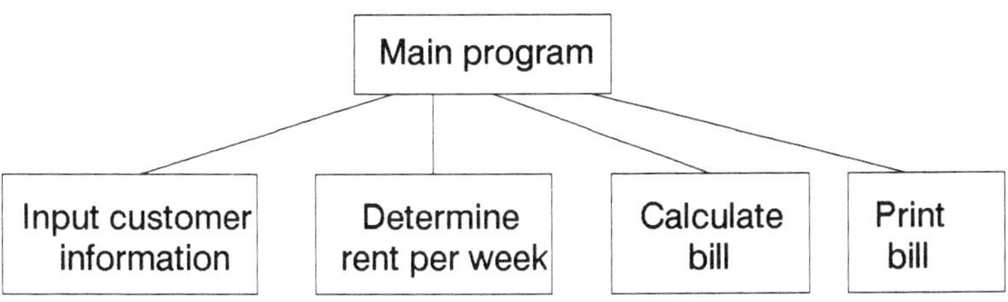

Pseudo code

The next stage in program development is to produce the pseudo code representation for each module. Pseudo code is a combination of restricted English and programming language terms which are used to describe the logic and steps to be performed within each module. While there are specific terms that have been formalised as pseudo code we will use be using very general language.

Using the TV Rental problem as an example, the pseudo code for the main program module would be

```
input customer information
determine rent per week
calculate bill
print bill
```

and for the 'calculate bill' module would be

```
bill = no of weeks rent due x weekly rental
```

These are relatively simple examples as our TV Rental problem is currently very simple, however the effectiveness of using pseudo code will become apparent in later chapters of this book.

The next stage in program development is to gradually convert the pseudo code representation of the module into program statements.

The program is then implemented by programming and testing one module. Once this module is working correctly then another module is added to it and again testing is carried out. In this way the complete program is built up and tested along the way.

Program testing

Perhaps at this stage mention should be made of how programs should be checked to ensure that they are working correctly.

The first step is to draw up a test strategy. Consideration should be given to the problem (not to the program). Determine the different situations that could arise in the problem and develop a set of data that will simulate each one. Now manually determine the expected outcome of each data set. Your program should then be tested for each data set. The program can only be considered to be working correctly if its output matches the manual outcomes.

In the TV Rental Program there is only one situation

- calculation of bill for colour TV.

Therefore if

rent is due for 3 weeks
and colour TV Rental is £3.60 per week
then bill = 3 x 3.60 = £10.80

If our program produced bills for both colour and black and white TV Rentals then two sets of test data would need to be constructed

- TEST 1 - Bill for colour TV
- TEST 2 - Bill for black and white TV.

2.2 Building Structured Programs In C

C is an ideal programming language for building structured programs as it was developed around the idea of combining functions together. Therefore it is possible to use a C function for each module. Although our TV Rental Program so far is, in theory, a monolithic solution, in terms of C it is a function called **main()**. All C programs have a **main()** function from which other functions are called. For example the TV Rental Program calls two library functions **scanf()** and **printf()**.

TV Rental Program using functions

By using functions it is possible to produce a better structure for our TV Rental Program. You may consider that it is so simple that this is unnecessary. However, it should be done in order that

- we develop good programming habits

- the extensions in later sections of this book are made more meaningful.

From the module relationship chart for the TV Rental Program it is obvious that we have five functions (one for each box), such that

Name	*Description*	*Data passed to function*	*Data returned from function*
main()	main program which calls the lower level functions	-	-
customer_input()	inputs customer information	-	customer no. no. of weeks rent due
weeks_rental()	determines rent per week	-	weekly rental
calc_bill()	calculate customers bill	no. of weeks rent due weekly rental	bill
print_bill()	prints customers bill	customer no no. of weeks rent due weekly rental bill	-

With the amount of the C programming language covered so far we can only return one value from a function. Therefore we cannot write the function customer_input() as it returns two values (customer_no and the no_of_weeks rent due). Hence, for the time being customer_input() will remain as part of the main program.

Consider the function **weeks_rental()**. In this case no data has to be passed to it, but the weekly rental has to be determined and passed back to the main program. As the value being passed back is of type **float**, the function also has to be of type **float** and has to be declared in the calling routine. Hence, the declaration is

```
float rent_per_week,weeks_rental();
```

and the function will be

```
float weeks_rental()  /*Determine rent per week*/
{
return(3.60);  /*Colour TV rental is 3.60*/
}
```

The outcome of this function is that **weeks_rental()** will be assigned the value contained within the **return** statement, in this case 3.60.

Therefore in the main program we will have the statement

```
rent_per_week = weeks_rental();
```

Hence the value returned to weeks_rental() will be assigned to rent_per_week. (NB this function will be expanded in later chapters.)

Now consider the function **print_bill**. In this case it requires to know the customer number, number of weeks rent due and the bill in order to print the TV rental bill. Therefore this data has to be passed to it and is referred to as the list of **function parameters**.

Hence the function print_bill is

```
print_bill(customer, weeks, rent, due)  /*Calculate and print the bill*/
int customer, weeks;
float rent, due;
{
    printf("\n\nTV RENTAL BILL");
    printf("\n\nCustomer number is %d", customer);
    printf("\nNumber of weeks rent due is %d", weeks);
    printf("\nRent per week is %.2f", rent);
    printf("\n\nRental due is %.2f\n\n", due);
}
```

The function print_bill has four parameters - customer, weeks, rent and due. It is necessary to indicate the data type of each of these parameters. This is called the parameter definition. The function body then follows enclosed in { }.

No return() is needed in this function as there are no values to be passed back to the calling function.

The call from main() to this function is

```
print_bill(customer_no, no_of_weeks, rent_per_week, bill);
```

The values in each of the variables are passed to the respective function parameters. For example, the value of customer_no is passed to customer.

Note that variable names cannot be used outside of the function in which they are declared. As such they are called **local variables** (i.e. they are local to the particular function). Usually to avoid confusion local variables should be given different names from those used in the calling routine.

The TV Rental Program re-written using functions is:

```
#include <stdio.h>

/* TV RENTAL BILLS - Version 2 - Using functions */

main()
{
   int no_of_weeks, customer_no;
   float rent_per_week, bill, weeks_rental(), calc_bill();

   /*Input customer number and number of weeks rent due*/
   printf("\nEnter customer number ");
   scanf("%4d",&customer_no);
   printf("Enter number of weeks rent due ");
   scanf("%2d",&no_of_weeks);

   /*Determine rent per week - colour TV is 3.60*/
   rent_per_week = weeks_rental();

   /*Calculate bill*/
   bill = calc_bill(no_of_weeks, rent_per_week);

   /*Print the bill*/
   print_bill(customer_no, no_of_weeks, rent_per_week, bill);
}

float weeks_rental()  /*Determine rent per week*/
{
   return(3.60); /*Colour TV rental is 3.60*/
}

float calc_bill(weeks, rent)   /*Calculate customers bill)*/
int weeks;
float rent;
{
   return(weeks * rent);
}

print_bill(customer, weeks, rent, due) /*Calculate and print the bill*/
int customer, weeks;
float rent, due;
```

```
{
   printf("\n\nTV RENTAL BILL");
   printf("\n\nCustomer number is %d", customer);
   printf("\nNumber of weeks rent due is %d", weeks);
   printf("\nRent per week is %.2f", rent);
   printf("\n\nRental due is %.2f\n\n", due);
}
```

Running this program will give:

Enter customer number **6666**
Enter number of weeks rent due **8**

TV RENTAL BILL

Customer number is 6666
Number of weeks rent due is 8
Rent per week is 3.60

Rental due is 28.80

Syntax of a function

A function takes the form

```
function_name(parameter_list if any)
parameter_list definitions if any
{
    program statements including the declaration of
         any local variables
              .
              .
              .
    return(variable_name) if the value of a variable
                  is to be returned to the
                  calling function
}
```

Note that

- if a function returns a decimal (i.e. float) value then (a) the function name must be preceded by the word float, and (b) it must be declared in the function that calls it.

- if a function has a parameter list then these must be defined immediately after the function name.
- for the present time any number of values may be passed to a function but only one may be returned from it.
- any variable names declared within the function are local to that function. Although the same name may be used in another function they are treated as two different variables.
- if the program runs but produces wrong answers then it is highly likely that the & has been left out of a scanf() statement.

Overall structure of a C program

Any C program that uses library input/output functions will take the form

```
#include <stdio.h>

    main()
    {
        program statements
    }

    function_1()
    {
        program statements
    }

    function_2()
    {
        program statements
    }
            .
            .
            .
```

2.3 Programming Exercises

1. Write a series of functions to perform the basic arithmetic functions (addition, subtraction, multiplication and division) on two numbers.

2. Write a program that inputs two numbers and outputs the result of their

addition, subtraction, multiplication and division. (NB use the functions written in question 1).

3. Write a function that inputs a character and outputs its ASCII equivalent.Test your function by writing a program to call your function.

3 Conditional Statements

Conditional statements are used to determine whether or not certain program statements should be executed.

As the TV Rental Program stands it assumes that all customers rent a colour television. The program is to be extended so that a bill is only produced for customers renting a colour television. Any other type of rental will result in an error message. This means that another input is required - c for colour TV rental. Hence the TV Rental Program will now be

```
#include <stdio.h>

/* TV RENTAL BILLS - Version 3
        - Bills ONLY for those renting colour TV s */
main()
{
    int no_of_weeks, customer_no;
    float rent_per_week, bill, weeks_rental(), calc_bill();

    /*Input customer number and number of weeks rent due*/
    printf("\nEnter customer number ");
    scanf("%4d",&customer_no);
    printf("Enter number of weeks rent due ");
    scanf("%2d",&no_of_weeks);

    /*Determine rent per week - colour TV is 3.60*/
    rent_per_week = weeks_rental();

    /*Calculate and print bill for acceptable TV types*/
    if (rent_per_week != 0)
      {
        /*Calculate bill*/
     bill = calc_bill(no_of_weeks, rent_per_week);

       /*Print the bill*/
       print_bill(customer_no, no_of_weeks, rent_per_week, bill);
      }
}
```

```
float weeks_rental()  /*Determine rent per week*/
{
    char tv_type;
    /*Input TV type*/
    printf("Enter type of rental - c for Colour TV");
    printf("\n                    o for other ");
    scanf("%s",&tv_type);

    /*Determine rent per week*/
    if (tv_type = = 'c')
      return(3.60); /*Colour TV rental is 3.60*/
    else
      {
      printf("\nProgram does not handle this type of rental\n");
      return(0);    /*Bill not to be calculated*/
      }
}

float calc_bill(weeks, rent)   /*Calculate customers bill)*/
int weeks;
float rent;
{
     return(weeks * rent);
}

print_bill(customer, weeks, rent, due)  /*Calculate and print the bill*/
int customer, weeks;
float rent, due;
{
     printf("\n\nTV RENTAL BILL");
     printf("\n\nCustomer number is %d", customer);
     printf("\nNumber of weeks rent due is %d", weeks);
     printf("\nRent per week is %.2f", rent);
     printf("\n\nRental due is %.2f\n\n", due);
}
```

Running the program gives:

```
Enter customer number 123
Enter number of weeks rent due 2
Enter type of rental - c for Colour TV
                       o for other c
```

```
TV RENTAL BILL

Customer number is 123
Number of weeks rent due is 2
Rent per week is 3.60

Rental due is 7.20


Enter customer number 678
Enter number of weeks rent due 3
Enter type of rental - c for Colour TV
                       o for other o

Program does not handle this type of rental


Enter customer number 1111
Enter number of weeks rent due 2
Enter type of rental - c for Colour TV
                       o for other g

Program does not handle this type of rental
```

The program has been changed in two respects. Firstly, the function weeks_rental() has been changed to input a character indicating type of rental (c for colour). Also an **if....else** statement is used to return a weekly rent of 3.60 if a colour TV is rented, otherwise, after printing an error message, a 0 is returned.

Secondly, an **if** statement precedes the calculation of a bill. Hence a bill is only calculated and output if the rent_per_week is not equal (! =) to zero (0 returned from weeks_rental indicates non-colour, hence not equal to zero indicates a colour television).

3.1 The if......else Statement

As can be seen in the TV Rental program the

```
if.....else.......
```

statement is used in order that certain program statements are obeyed only if certain conditions hold. The general form of this statement is

```
if (<conditional_expression>)
        statement_1;
    else
        statement_2;
```

The above program instructions are interpreted as

```
if the <conditional_expression> is TRUE
        then statement_1 is executed
However, if the <conditional_expression> is FALSE
        then statement_2 is executed.
```

The <conditional_expression> is an expression containing variables, possibly arithmetic operators, and at least one of the following logical operators

>	greater than	>=	greater than or equal to
<	less than	<=	less than or equal to
==	equal	!=	not equal

Examples of conditional expressions are

```
rent_per_week != 0

tv_type == 'c'

min > max

s == limit + excess
```

A number of <conditional_expressions> can be combined using the logical operators

&&	logical AND
||	logical OR
!	NOT

For example,

```
mean >10 && mean < 20

min > max && number == 0
```

An examples of an **if....else** statement is

```
if (ball = = 'red')
  point = 1;
else
  point = 2;
```

In this case if the value of ball is red then point will take the value 1. On the other hand, if the value of the ball is **not** red then point takes the value 2.

3.2 Special Cases Of if..... else.... Statement

There are a number of variations of the **if...else...** statement. The syntax of these are

```
if (<conditional_expression>)
  statement_1;
```

In this case statement_1 is only obeyed if the <conditional_expression> is TRUE.

If it is FALSE the next program statement is obeyed. An example of this is

```
if (paper= = 'A4')
  printf("\nPut a sheet of paper in your printer");
```

In this case the message is only output if the value of paper is A4.

```
if (<conditional_expression>)
{
  statement_1;
  statement_2;
     .
     .
     .
  statement_n;
}
```

In this case, if the <conditional_expression> is TRUE then all the statements enclosed in the {} are obeyed.

If the <conditional_expression> is FALSE the next program statement is obeyed (i.e. the statement following the }).

An example of this can be seen in the main() function of the TV Rental Program.

```
if (rent_per_week != 0)
{
  /*Calculate bill*/
  bill = calc_bill(no_of_weeks, rent_per_week);

  /*Print the bill*/
  print_bill(customer_no, no_of_weeks, rent_per_week, bill);
}
```

In this case the customer's bill is only calculated and printed if the rent_per_week is non-zero.

```
if (<conditional_expression>)
{
   statement_1;
   statement_2;
      .
      .
      .
   statement_n;
}
else
   statemnt_1_1;
```

In this case, if the <conditional_expression> is TRUE then all the statements enclosed in the {} are obeyed.

However, if the <conditional_expression> is FALSE then the statement following the else is obeyed.

An example of this form of the **if.....else** statement is

```
if (number = 0)
{
   sum = sum + number;
   sum_square = sum_square + number* number;
}
else
   printf("\nINVALID NUMBER \nRe-enter number");
```

In this case if the value of number is positive then the values of sum and sum_square are calculated. However, if the value of number is negative the error message is printed.

```
if (<conditional_expression>)
{
   statement_1;
   statement_2;
      .
   statement_n;
}
else
{
   statement_1_1;
   statement_1_2;
      .
   statement_1_n;
}
```

An example of this form of the **if.....else** statement is

```
if (credit == 'y')
{
   printf("\nTotal bill is %.2f", bill);
   printf("\n\nPayment required within 30 days");
}
else
{
   bill = bill - 0.1 * bill
   printf("\nWith 10 per cent discount for cash payment");
   printf("\nTotal bill is %.2f", bill);
}
```

In this case a discount is only given if the customer does not get credit.

In all cases with an **if....else...** statement, once the appropriate part of the statement has been obeyed, the next statement obeyed is the next statement in the program.

3.3 A Shorthand Version Of A Simple if....else... Statement

Consider the example

```
if   (n>m)
           max = n;
      else
           max = m;
```

In C another way of writing this is

```
max (n>m)?n:m;
```

That is, if (n>m) is TRUE, max takes the value of n. However, if (n>m) is FALSE, max takes the value of m.

The general syntax of this statement is

```
variable_name = (<conditional_expression>)?
                                        variable_1:variable_2;
```

3.4 Programming Exercises

From now on all programming exercises should be written using functions.

1. Write a program that will input a whole number. A message will then be output indicating whether or not the number is a multiple of 3.

2. Write a program that will input a temperature followed by an indication as to whether it is degrees Celsius or Fahrenheit. The program will then calculate and output the temperature on the other degree scale (i.e. a temperature in degrees Celsius will be converted to Fahrenheit and one in Fahrenheit will be converted to Celsius).

3. Write a program that will input a single character. A message will be output indicating whether or not the character was a digit.

3.5 The if....else if.... Statement

Returning to the TV Rental Program. At present it only produces bills for colour TVs. It will now be extended to allow for both colour televisions and black and white televisions. The rental for a colour television is £3.60 and that for a black and white television is £1.75. Hence, as it is necessary to distinguish between the different television types, tv_type will now have the value c for colour and b for black and white. In all other cases an error message will be output and a bill will not be produced.

As this extension affects the determination of the weeks rental, only the body of the function weeks_rental() will need altering to

```
        if (tv_type = = 'c')
              return(3.60);  /*Colour TV rental is 3.60*/
            else if (tv_type = = 'b')
                return(1.75);  /*Black and white TV rental is 1.75*/
              else
                {
                printf("\nProgram does not handle this type of rental\n");
                return(0);    /*Bill not to be calculated*/
                }
```

and the complete program is

```
#include < stdio.h >

/* TV RENTAL BILLS - Version 4
  - Bills for those renting colour and
    black and white TV s */

main()
{
    int no_of_weeks, customer_no;
    float rent_per_week, bill, weeks_rental(), calc_bill();

    /*Input customer number and number of weeks rent due*/
    printf("\nEnter customer number ");
    scanf("%4d",&customer_no);
    printf("Enter number of weeks rent due ");
    scanf("%2d",&no_of_weeks);

    /*Determine rent per week - colour TV is 3.60*/
    rent_per_week = weeks_rental();

    /*Calculate and print bill for acceptable TV types*/
    if (rent_per_week ! = 0)
    {
        /*Calculate bill*/
        bill = calc_bill(no_of_weeks, rent_per_week);

        /*Print the bill*/
        print_bill(customer_no, no_of_weeks, rent_per_week, bill);
    }
}
```

```
float weeks_rental()   /*Determine rent per week*/
{
    char tv_type;

    /*Input TV type*/
    printf("Enter type of rental - c for Colour TV");
    printf("\n                   b for Black and white TV");
    printf("\n                   o for other ");
    scanf("%s",&tv_type);

    /*Determine rent per week*/
    if (tv_type = = 'c')
        return(3.60);  /*Colour TV rental is 3.60*/
    else if (tv_type = = 'b')
            return(1.75);  /*Black and white TV rental is 1.75*/
        else
        {
            printf("\nProgram does not handle this type of rental\n");
            return(0);     /*Bill not to be calculated*/
        }
}

float calc_bill(weeks, rent)    /*Calculate customers bill)*/
int weeks;
float rent;
{
    return(weeks * rent);
}

print_bill(customer, weeks, rent, due)  /*Calculate and print the bill*/
int customer, weeks;
float rent, due;
{
    printf("\n\nTV RENTAL BILL");
    printf("\n\nCustomer number is %d", customer);
    printf("\nNumber of weeks rent due is %d", weeks);
    printf("\nRent per week is %.2f", rent);
    printf("\n\nRental due is %.2f\n\n", due);
}
```

Running this program now gives:

Enter customer number **1234**
Enter number of weeks rent due **1**
Enter type of rental - c for Colour TV
b for Black and white TV
o for other **b**

TV RENTAL BILL

Customer number is 1234
Number of weeks rent due is 1
Rent per week is 1.75

Rental due is 1.75

Enter customer number **3232**
Enter number of weeks rent due **4**
Enter type of rental - c for Colour TV
b for Black and white TV
o for other **o**

Program does not handle this type of rental

Enter customer nmber **3333**
Enter number of weeks rent due **6**
Enter type of rental - c for Colour TV
b for Black and white TV
o for other **c**

TV RENTAL BILL

Customer number is 3333
Number of weeks rent due is 6
Rent per week is 3.60

Rental due is 21.60

The new statement that was introduced was the **if.....else if...** which has the following syntax

```
if (<conditional_expression>)
        statement_1;
    else if (<conditional_expression>)
            statement_2;
        else if (<conditional_expression>)
                statement_3;
            else statement_4;
```

Any of the above statement_s above can be replaced by a group of statements enclosed in {}.

As soon as a <conditional_expression> is found to be TRUE the statement(s) immediately following it is obeyed. Control is then passed to the program statement following the **if...else if...** statement.

If none of the <conditional_expression>s are TRUE then the statement(s) following the last else is obeyed.

By introducing a third type of rental (i.e. a video) into our TV Rental Program all that has to be changed is the **if....else if....** statement in the function weeks_rental() to

```
if (tv_type == 'c')
      return(3.60); /*Colour TV rental is 3.60*/
    else if (tv_type == 'b')
        return(1.75); /*Black and white TV rental is 1.75*/
      else if (tv_type == 'v')
            return(1.50); /*Video rental is 1.50*/
          else
            {
            printf("\n Program does not handle this type of rental\n");
            return(0);    /*Bill not to be calculated*/
            }
```

Incorporating these changes in the TV Rental Program gives

```
#include <stdio.h>

/* TV RENTAL BILLS - Version 5
- Bills for those renting colour and
black and white TVs and videos*/

main()
{
    int no_of_weeks, customer_no;
    float rent_per_week, bill, weeks_rental(), calc_bill();
```

```
    /*Input customer number and number of weeks rent due*/
    printf("\nEnter customer number ");
    scanf("%4d",&customer_no);
    printf("Enter number of weeks rent due ");
    scanf("%2d",&no_of_weeks);

    /*Determine rent per week - colour TV is 3.60*/
    rent_per_week = weeks_rental();

    /*Calculate and print bill for acceptable TV types*/
    if (rent_per_week != 0)
    {
        /*Calculate bill*/
        bill = calc_bill(no_of_weeks, rent_per_week);

        /*Print the bill*/
        print_bill(customer_no, no_of_weeks, rent_per_week, bill);
    }
}

float weeks_rental()   /*Determine rent per week*/
{
    char tv_type;

    /*Input TV type*/
    printf("Enter type of rental - c for Colour TV");
    printf("\n                     b for Black and white TV");
    printf("\n                     v for Video");
    printf("\n                     o for other ");
    scanf("%s",&tv_type);

    /*Determine rent per week*/
    if (tv_type == 'c')
        return(3.60); /*Colour TV rental is 3.60*/
        else if (tv_type == 'b')
            return(1.75); /*Black and white TV rental is 1.75*/
            else if (tv_type == 'v')
                return(1.50); /*Video rental is 1.50*/
                else
                {
                  printf("\nProgram does not handle this type of rental\n");
                  return(0);    /*Bill not to be calculated*/
                }
}
```

```
float calc_bill(weeks, rent)    /*Calculate customers bill)*/
int weeks;
float rent;
{
    return(weeks * rent);
}

print_bill(customer, weeks, rent, due) /*Calculate and print the bill*/
int customer, weeks;
float rent, due;
{
    printf("\n\nTV RENTAL BILL");
    printf("\n\nCustomer number is %d", customer);
    printf("\nNumber of weeks rent due is %d", weeks);
    printf("\nRent per week is %.2f", rent);
    printf("\n\nRental due is %.2f\n\n", due);
}
```

Running this program gives:

```
Enter customer number 630
Enter number of weeks rent due 1
Enter type of rental - c for Colour TV
                       b for Black and white TV
                       v for Video
                       o for other c


TV RENTAL BILL

Customer number is 630
Number of weeks rent due is 1
Rent per week is 3.60

Rental due is 3.60


Enter customer number 645
Enter number of weeks rent due 5
Enter type of rental - c for Colour TV
                       b for Black and white TV
                       v for Video
                       o for other v
```

```
TV RENTAL BILL

Customer number is 645
Number of weeks rent due is 5
Rent per week is 1.50

Rental due is 7.50


Enter customer number 4444
Enter number of weeks rent due 2
Enter type of rental - c for Colour TV
                       b for Black and white TV
                       v for Video
                       o for other b


TV RENTAL BILL

Customer number is 4444
Number of weeks rent due is 2
Rent per week is 1.75

Rental due is 3.50


Enter customer number 4321
Enter number of weeks rent due 1
Entr type of rental - c for Colour TV
                      b for Black and white TV
                      v for Video
                      o for other m

Program does not handle this type of rental
```

By now it should be obvious that the **if....else if....** statement can be very cumbersome, both to write and to follow through. Therefore, once there are more than three options it is better to use a switch statement.

3.6 The Switch Statement

The switch statement is effectively an **if...else if...** statement that will handle any number of options without becoming cumbersome or unreadable.

Consider the **if...else if...** statement in the TV Rental Program. It can be replaced by

```
    switch (tv_type)
{
    case 'c': /*Colour TV rental is 3.60*/
            return(3.60);
    case 'b': /*Black and white TV rental is 1.75*/
            return(1.75);
    case 'v': /*Video rental is 1.50*/
            return(1.50);
    default : /*Illegal input for tv_type*/
            printf("\nProgram does not handle this type of rental\n");
            return(0);
    }
```

Altering the TV Rental Program to use a switch statement gives

```
#include <stdio.h>

/* TV RENTAL BILLS - Version 6
  - Bills for those renting colour and
     black and white TV s and videos*/

main()
{
    int no_of_weeks, customer_no;
    float rent_per_week, bill, weeks_rental(), calc_bill();

    /*Input customer number and number of weeks rent due*/
    printf("\nEnter customer number ");
    scanf("%4d",&customer_no);
    printf("Enter number of weeks rent due ");
    scanf("%2d",&no_of_weeks);

    /*Determine rent per week - colour TV is 3.60*/
    rent_per_week = weeks_rental();

    /*Calculate and print bill for acceptable TV types*/
    if (rent_per_week != 0)
    {
        /*Calculate bill*/
        bill = calc_bill(no_of_weeks, rent_per_week);
```

```
        /*Print the bill*/
        print_bill(customer_no, no_of_weeks, rent_per_week, bill);
    }
}

float weeks_rental()   /*Determine rent per week*/
{
    char tv_type;

    /*Input TV type*/
    printf("Enter type of rental - c for Colour TV");
    printf("\n                    b for Black and white TV");
    printf("\n                    v for Video");
    printf("\n                    o for other ");
    scanf("%s",&tv_type);

    /*Determine rent per week*/
    switch (tv_type)
    {
    case 'c': /*Colour TV rental is 3.60*/
            return(3.60);
    case 'b': /*Black and white TV rental is 1.75*/
            return(1.75);
    case 'v': /*Video rental is 1.50*/
            return(1.50);
    default : /*Illegal input for tv_type*/
            printf("\nProgram does not handle this type of rental\n");
            return(0)
    }
}

float calc_bill(weeks, rent)    /*Calculate customers bill)*/
int weeks;
float rent;
{
    return(weeks * rent);
}

print_bill(customer, weeks, rent, due)  /*Calculate and print the bill*/
int customer, weeks;
float rent, due;
{
    printf("\n\nTV RENTAL BILL");
    printf("\n\nCustomer number is %d", customer);
```

```
    printf("\nNumber of weeks rent due is %d", weeks);
    printf("\nRent per week is %.2f", rent);
    printf("\n\nRental due is %.2f\n\n", due);
}
```

Running this program gives:

```
Enter customer number 1234
Enter number of weeks rent due 1
Enter type of rental - c for Colour TV
                       b for Black and white TV
                       v for Video
                       o for other o

Program does not handle this type of rental


Enter customer number 2000
Enter number of weeks rent due 2
Enter type of rental - c for Colour TV
                       b for Black and white TV
                       v for Video
                       o for other b


TV RENTAL BILL

Customer number is 2000
Number of weeks rent due is 2
Rent per week is 1.75

Rental due is 3.50


Enter customer number 3100
Enter number of weeks rent due 1
Enter type of rental - c for Colour TV
                       b for Black and white TV
                       v for Video
                       o for other v


TV RENTAL BILL
```

```
Customer number is 3100
Number of weeks rent due is 1
Rent per week is 1.50
Rental due is 1.50


Enter customer number 4000
Enter number of weeks rent due 2
Enter type of rental - c for Colour TV
                       b for Black and white TV
                       v for Video
                       o for other c


TV RENTAL BILL

Customer number is 4000
Number of weeks rent due is 2
Rent per week is 3.60

Rental due is 7.20
```

The general syntax of the switch statement is

```
switch (<arithmetic_expression>)
  {
  case 'value':       .
                      .
        program statements;
                      .
        break;
  case 'value':       .
                      .
        program statements;
                      .
        break;
    .
    .
  default:            .
                      .
        program statements;
                      .
        break;
  }
```

The <arithmetic_expression> is evaluated. If its value is contained within the **switch** statement then the program statements following its **case** are obeyed. If the value does not exist the program statements following the **default** are obeyed. When there is no **default** in the switch statement control is passed to the program statement following the switch statement.

Once program statements start being obeyed inside a **switch** statement, they will continue being obeyed unless they hit a statement that jumps control out of the switch statement. Two such statements are **return()** which returns program control to the calling function and **break** which passes control to the statement following the switch statement.

Notes on the switch statement

- <arithmetic_expression> must give an integer result or be a single character.
- each **case** must be labelled by a constant integer, character or <arithmetic_expression> (NB quotes are only required around character values).
- each **case** must be unique.
- **default** is optional.
- **case** s and **default** can occur in any order.

3.7 Programming Exercises

1. Write a program to input two numbers and then display the following menu

    1 Sum of two numbers
    2 Subtract the second number from the first
    3 Multiply the two numbers together
    4 Divide the first number by the second
    5 None of the above

The program will then produce the output selected by the user from the menu.

2. Write a function called look_up which determines the discount available depending on the quantity of goods ordered. Hence if the discount table is

Quantity	Discount %
1	0
2 - 4	5
5 or more	10

then for quantity equal to 3, the look_up function will return the value 5.

3. Write a program to input the cost of an item and the number of items bought. Using the look_up function from question 2 the program should calculate and print the total cost of the items, taking into account any quantity discount.

4 Program Loops

Often in a program it is desirable to repeat certain sections of the code. One way of doing this would be to repeat the appropriate program instructions. However, this would lead to cumbersome programs. Using C sections of a program can be repeated using **for**, **while** and **do** loops.

4.1 The for.... Statement

Consider our TV Rental Program. Currently it only produces one bill. It will now be extended to produce more than one bill, this means that before entering any information about a customer, the number of bills to be processed will require to be input.

Hence the changes required in the TV Rental program will be

- input number of bills to be processed
- repeat the code that processes the bills the required number of times

Both these changes are made to main() which becomes

```
main()
{
    int no_of_weeks, customer_no;
    int no_of_bills, i;
    float rent_per_week, bill, weeks_rental(), calc_bill();

    /*Input number of bills to be produced*/
    printf("How many bills are to be produced? ");
    scanf("%4d",&no_of_bills);

    /*Produce required number of bills*/
    for (i=1; i<=no_of_bills; ++i)
    {

        /*Input customer number and number of weeks rent due*/
        printf("\nEnter customer number ");
        scanf("%4d",&customer_no);
```

```
        printf("Enter number of weeks rent due ");
        scanf("%2d",&no_of_weeks);

        /*Determine rent per week - colour TV is 3.60*/
        rent_per_week = weeks_rental();

        /*Calculate and print bill for acceptable TV types*/
        if (rent_per_week != 0)
        {
            /*Calculate bill*/
            bill = calc_bill(no_of_weeks, rent_per_week);

            /*Print the bill*/
            print_bill(customer_no, no_of_weeks, rent_per_week, bill);
        }
    }
}
```

In this case we are using the statement

```
for (i=1; i<=no_of_bills; ++i)
 {
     program statements that are to be repeated
 }
```

i is just a control variable which is given the initial value of 1. The program statements inside the {} are repeated as long as

```
i<=no_of_bills
```

This implies that the value of i is changing. In this case i is increased by 1 (++i) every time the loop is repeated.

At this point it is perhaps worth pointing out that C is full of shorthand notation. For example

C shorthand	*Meaning*
++i	increment i by 1 **before** using its value
i++	increment i by 1 **after** using its value
--i	decrement i by 1 **before** using its value
i--	decrement i by 1 **after** using its value

With the above changes to **main()** the TV Rental Program becomes

```
#include <stdio.h>

/* TV RENTAL BILLS - Version 7
- Production of a specified number of
  bills for those renting colour and
  black and white TV s and videos*/

main()
{
    int no_of_weeks, customer_no;
    int no_of_bills, i;
    float rent_per_week, bill, weeks_rental(), calc_bill();

    /*Input number of bills to be produced*/
    printf("How many bills are to be produced? ");
    scanf("%4d",&no_of_bills);

    /*Produce required number of bills*/
    for (i=1; i<=no_of_bills; ++i)
    {

        /*Input customer number and number of weeks rent due*/
        printf("\nEnter customer number ");
        scanf("%4d",&customer_no);
        printf("Enter number of weeks rent due ");
        scanf("%2d",&no_of_weeks);

        /*Determine rent per week - colour TV is 3.60*/
        rent_per_week = weeks_rental();

        /*Calculate and print bill for acceptable TV types*/
        if (rent_per_week != 0)
        {
            /*Calculate bill*/
            bill = calc_bill(no_of_weeks, rent_per_week);

            /*Print the bill*/
            print_bill(customer_no, no_of_weeks, rent_per_week, bill);
        }
    }
}
```

```
float weeks_rental()  /*Determine rent per week*/
{
    char tv_type;

    /*Input TV type*/
    printf("Enter type of rental - c for Colour TV");
    printf("\n                    b for Black and white TV");
    printf("\n                    v for Video");
    printf("\n                    o for other ");
    scanf("%s",&tv_type);

    /*Determine rent per week*/
    switch (tv_type)
    {
    case 'c': /*Colour TV rental is 3.60*/
         return(3.60);
    case 'b': /*Black and white TV rental is 1.75*/
         return(1.75);
    case 'v': /*Video rental i 1.50*/
         return(1.50);
    default : /*Illegal input for tv_type*/
         printf("\nProgram does not handle this type of rental\n");
         return(0);
    }
}

float calc_bill(weeks, rent)   /*Calculate customers bill)*/
int weeks;
float rent;
{
    return(weeks * rent);
}

print_bill(customer, weeks, rent, due)  /*Calculate and print the bill*/
int customer, weeks;
float rent, due;
{
    printf("\n\nTV RENTAL BILL");
    printf("\n\nCustomer number is %d", customer);
    printf("\nNumber of weeks rent due is %d", weeks);
    printf("\nRent per week is %.2f", rent);
    printf("\n\nRental due is %.2f\n\n", due);
}
```

Running this program gives:

How many bills are to be produced? **5**

Enter customer number **1333**
Enter number of weeks rent due **4**
Enter type of rental - c for Colour TV
b for Black and white TV
v for Video
o for other **b**

TV RENTAL BILL

Customer number is 1333
Number of weeks rent due is 4
Rent per week is 1.75

Rental due is 7.00

Enter customer number **3444**
Enter number of weeks rent due **5**
Enter type of rental - c for Colour TV
b for Black and white TV
v for Video
o for other **c**

TV RENTAL BILL

Customer number is 3444
Number of weeks rent due is 5
Rent per week is 3.60

Rental due is 18.00

Enter customer number **5555**
Enter number of weeks rent due **1**
Enter type of rental - c for Colour TV
b for Black and white TV
v for Video
o for other **o**

```
Program does not handle this type of rental

Enter customer number 7000
Enter number of weeks rent due 1
Enter type of rental - c for Colour TV
                       b for Black and white TV
                       v for Video
                       o for other b


TV RENTAL BILL

Customer number is 7000
Number of weeks rent due is 1
Rent per week is 1.75

Rental due is 1.75


Enter customer number 99
Enter number of weeks rent due 0
Enter type of rental - c for Colour TV
                       b for Black and white TV
                       v for Video
                       o for other c


TV RENTAL BILL

Customer number is 99
Number of weeks rent due is 0
Rent per week is 3.60

Rental due is 0.00
```

The general syntax of the **for** statement is

```
for (initial_condition; terminating_condition; increment)
      program_statement;
```

where the

initial_condition is an assignment statement or function used to set the starting value for the loop control variable.

terminating_condition is a relational expression used to determine when the loop will finish. The loop is repeated so long as the terminating condition is TRUE.

increment is an assignment statement or function used to indicate how the loop control variable will change for every repeat of the loop.
For example,

```
for (i=1; i< =100; + +i)
    printf("\ni=%d",i);
```

Here i takes the initial value 1 and is increased by 1 every time the loop is obeyed, so long as i is < = 100. Hence the output from this section of program is

```
i=1
i=2
 .
 .
i=100
```

The statements

```
for (x=1000; x! =500; x=x-50)
    printf("\nx=%d",x);
```

indicate that x has an initial value of 1000 which is decreased by 50 every time the loop is repeated so long as x is not equal to 500. Hence the output from this program section is

```
x=1000
x=950
  .
  .
x=550
```

There are a number of variations of the program loop.

Repeating multiple statements

In this case the general syntax is

```
for (initial_condition; terminating_condition; increment)
{
    program_statement_1;
    program_statement_2;
          .
          .
          .
    program_statement_n;
}
```

For example,

```
for (i=1; i< =100; + +i)
{
    square_root = sqrt(i);
    printf("\nThesquareroot of%dis%f",i,square_root);
}
```

NB The function sqrt() is a library function which computes the square root of its parameter.

In this case the two statements enclosed in { } are repeated the appropriate number of times.

Multiple loop variables

For example,

```
for (i=0, y=0; i< =100; + +i, y=i+2)
{
          .
          .
          .
}
```

In this case i and y are set to 0 at the start of the loop. Each time the loop is repeated i is increased by 1 and y is set equal to i+2. The loop is repeated until i< =100.

It is also possible to change the value of the loop variable in one of the statements inside the loop. For example,

```
for (x=0, num=0; x+num!=100; ++x)
{
        .
        .
        num =
        .
        .
}
```

Missing loop definitions

The initial value of the loop control variable can be set before the for statement is encountered. For example,

```
scanf("%d",&i);
for (; i<100; ++i)
{
    .
    .
    .
}
```

It is also possible to increment the loop control variable inside the loop. For example,

```
for (i=10; i<100;)
{
   printf("\n%d %d %d", i, i*i, i*i*i);
   ++i;
}
```

By removing the terminating condition we have an infinite loop. For example,

```
for (i=0;;++i)
{
    .
    .
}
```

or even

```
for (;;)
{
  .
  .
}
```

However, it is bad programming practice to use infinite loops.

No following program statements

Sometimes in programs it is necessary to slow down the processing speed. One way of doing this is to introduce a time delay. For example,

```
for (i=0; i< =1000; + +i);
```

That is, a for statement without any following program statements.

4.2 The while.... Statement

While the TV Rental Program will now produce a number of bills it is inconvenient to have to count them before running the program. It would be much better if the user could just indicate whether or not there are any more bills to be produced. This could be achieved by:

- using a **while** statement to control the loop.
- asking the user if another bill is to be produced after printing a bill.

Again these changes only effect the **main()** function which will become

```
main()
{
    int no_of_weeks, customer_no;
    float rent_per_week, bill, weeks_rental(), calc_bill();
    char another_bill;

    /*Set initial value of another_bill to yes*/
    another_bill='y';

    /*Produce required number of bills*/
    while (another_bill = = 'y')
      {
```

```
        /*Input customer number and number of weeks rent due*/
        printf("\nEnter customer number ");
        scanf("%4d",&customer_no);
        printf("Enter number of weeks rent due ");
        scanf("%2d",&no_of_weeks);

        /*Determine rent per week - colour TV is 3.60*/
        rent_per_week = weeks_rental();

        /*Calculate and print bill for acceptable TV types*/
        if (rent_per_week != 0)
        {
            /*Calculate bill*/
            bill = calc_bill(no_of_weeks, rent_per_week);

            /*Print the bill*/
            print_bill(customer_no, no_of_weeks, rent_per_week, bill);
        }

        /*Another bill*/
        printf("Is there another bill to be processed (y or n)? ");
        scanf("%s",&another_bill);
    }
}
```

So long as the variable another_bill has the value 'y' the program statements inside the loop will be obeyed. Once another bill is not equal to 'y' the loop is terminated. As another_bill is initialised to 'y' the loop is obeyed at least once.

The TV Rental Program is now

```
#include <stdio.h>

/* TV RENTAL BILLS - Version 8
  - Production of an UNSPECIFIED number of
    bills for those renting colour and
     black and white TV s and videos*/

main()
{
    int no_of_weeks, customer_no;
    float rent_per_week, bill, weeks_rental(), calc_bill();
    char another_bill;
```

```
    /*Set initial value of another_bill to yes*/
    another_bill = 'y';

    /*Produce required number of bills*/
    while (another_bill = = 'y')
    {

        /*Input customer number and number of weeks rent due*/
        printf("\nEnter customer number ");
        scanf("%4d",&customer_no);
        printf("Enter number of weeks rent due ");
        scanf("%2d",&no_of_weeks);

        /*Determine rent per week - colour TV is 3.60*/
        rent_per_week = weeks_rental();

        /*Calculate and print bill for acceptable TV types*/
        if (rent_per_week ! = 0)
        {
            /*Calculate bill*/
            bill = calc_bill(no_of_weeks, rent_per_week);

            /*Print the bill*/
            print_bill(customer_no, no_of_weeks, rent_per_week, bill);
        }

        /*Another bill*/
        printf("Is there another bill to be processed (y or n)? ");
        scanf("%s",&another_bill);
    }
}

float weeks_rental()   /*Determine rent per week*/
{
    char tv_type;

    /*Input TV type*/
    printf("Enter type of rental - c for Colour TV");
    printf("\n                    b for Black and white TV");
    printf("\n                    v for Video");
    printf("\n                    o for other ");
    scanf("%s",&tv_type);
```

```
    /*Determine rent per week*/
    switch (tv_type)
    {
    case 'c': /*Colour TV rental is 3.60*/
        return(3.60);
    case 'b': /*Black and white TV rental is 1.75*/
        return(1.75);
    case 'v': /*Video rental is 1.50*/
        return(1.50);
    default : /*Illegal input for tv_type*/
        printf("\nProgram does not handle this type of rental\n");
        return(0);
    }
}

float calc_bill(weeks, rent)    /*Calculate customers bill)*/
int weeks;
float rent;
{
    return(weeks * rent);
}

print_bill(customer, weeks, rent, due)  /*Calculate and print the bill*/
int customer, weeks;
float rent, due;
{
    printf("\n\nTV RENTAL BILL");
    printf("\n\nCustomer number is %d", customer);
    printf("\nNumber of weeks rent due is %d", weeks);
    printf("\nRent per week is %.2f", rent);
    printf("\n\nRental due is %.2f\n\n", due);
}
```

Running this program gives:

Enter customer number **4000**
Enter number of weeks rent due **2**
Enter type of rental - c for Colour TV
                        b for Black and white TV
                        v for Video
                        o for other **c**

```
TV RENTAL BILL

Customer number is 4000
Number of weeks rent due is 2
Rent per week is 3.60

Rental due is 7.20

Is there another bill to be processed (y or n)? y

Enter customer number 46
Enter number of weeks rent due 2
Enter type of rental - c for Colour TV
                       b for Black and white TV
                       v for Video
                       o for other v


TV RENTAL BILL

Customer number is 46
Number of weeks rent due is 2
Rent per week is 1.50

Rental due is 3.00

Is there another bill to be processed (y or n)? n
```

The general syntax of the **while** statement is

```
while ( < conditional_expression > )
      program_statement;
```

or

```
while ( < condtional_expression > )
{
      program_statement_1;
      program_statement_2;
            .
            .
      program_statement_n;
}
```

If the <conditional_expression> is TRUE then the following program statement or block of statements (enclosed in {}) are performed.

If the <conditional_expression> is FALSE the program statement(s) within the loop are not performed.

NB As the <conditional_expression> is checked at the start of the **while** loop it is possible for it never to be performed (i.e. if the conditional_expression is FALSE).

4.3 for... Or while... ?

Consider the following **while** statement.

```
while (another_no = 'y')
{
        .
    scanf("%d",&another_no);
        .
}
```

This is in fact equivalent to the following statement

```
for (i=1; another_no!='y'; ++i)
{
        .
    scanf("%d",&another_no);
        .
}
```

There are no hard and fast rules as to when to use a **while** statement and when to use a **for** statement. Just use the statement that seems most appropriate to the particular situation.

4.4 The do......while Statement

The **do....while** statement provides yet another means of repeating parts of a program. The general syntax is

```
do
    program_statement;
while (<conditional_expression>);
```

or

```
do
        {
          program_statement_1;
          program_statement_2;
                  .
          program_statement_n;
        }
        while (<conditional_expression>);
```

A **do....while** loop is always obeyed at least once as the <conditional_expression> is tested at the end of the loop. If the <conditional_expression> is TRUE the loop is repeated, otherwise it is terminated.

One advantage of using the **do....while** statement over the **while** statement is that as the loop is always obeyed at least once, no initialisation of the <conditional_expression> is required. For example in our TV Rental Program another_bill would not have to be set to 'y' at the beginning. Instead the **main()** function would be

```
main()
{
   int no_of_weeks, customer_no;
   float rent_per_week, bill, weeks_rental(), calc_bill();
   char another_bill;

   /*Produce required number of bills*/
   do
   {

      /*Input customer number and number of weeks rent due*/
      printf("\nEnter customer number ");
      scanf("%4d",&customer_no);
      printf("Enter number of weeks rent due ");
      scanf("%2d",&no_of_weeks);

      /*Determine rent per week - colour TV is 3.60*/
      rent_per_week = weeks_rental();

      /*Calculate and print bill for acceptable TV types*/
      if (rent_per_week != 0)
      {
         /*Calculate bill*/
         bill = calc_bill(no_of_weeks, rent_per_week);
```

```
        /*Print the bill*/
        print_bill(customer_no, no_of_weeks, rent_per_week, bill);
      }

      /*Another bill*/
      printf("Is there another bill to be processed (y or n)? ");
      scanf("%s",&another_bill);
      }
      while(another_bill = = 'y');
}
```

Hence the TV Rental Program converted to use a **do....while** statement is

```
#include <stdio.h>

/* TV RENTAL BILLS - Version 9
  - Production of an UNSPECIFIED number of
    bills for those renting colour and
    black and white TV s and videos*/

main()
{
    int no_of_weeks, customer_no;
    float rent_per_week, bill, weeks_rental(), calc_bill();
    char another_bill;

    /*Produce required number of bills*/
    do
          {

      /*Input customer number and number of weeks rent due*/
      printf("\nEnter customer number ");
      scanf("%4d",&customer_no);
      printf("Enter number of weeks rent due ");
      scanf("%2d",&no_of_weeks);

      /*Determine rent per week - colour TV is 3.60*/
      rent_per_week = weeks_rental();

      /*Calculate and print bill for acceptable TV types*/
      if (rent_per_week ! = 0)
      {
        /*Calculate bill*/
        bill = calc_bill(no_of_weeks, rent_per_week);
```

```
        /*Print the bill*/
        print_bill(customer_no, no_of_weeks, rent_per_week, bill);
      }

      /*Another bill*/
      printf("Is there another bill to be processed (y or n)? ");
      scanf("%s",&another_bill);
      }
      while(another_bill = = 'y');
}

float weeks_rental()   /*Determine rent per week*/
{
    char tv_type;

    /*Input TV type*/
    printf("Enter type of rental - c for Colour TV");
    printf("\n                    b for Black and white TV");
    printf("\n                    v for Video");
    rintf("\n                   o for other ");
    scanf("%s",&tv_type);

    /*Determine rent per week*/
    switch (tv_type)
    {
    case 'c': /*Colour TV rental is 3.60*/
          return(3.60);
    case 'b': /*Black and white TV rental is 1.75*/
          return(1.75);
    case 'v': /*Video rental is 1.50*/
          return(1.50);
    default : /*Illegal input for tv_type*/
          printf("\nProgram does not handle this type of rental\n");
          return(0);
    }
}

float calc_bill(weeks, rent)    /*Calculate customers bill)*/
int weeks;
float rent;
{
    return(weeks * rent);
}
```

```
print_bill(customer, weeks, rent, due)  /*Calculate and print the bill*/
int customer, weeks;
float rent, due;
{
    printf("\n\nTV RENTAL BILL");
    printf("\n\nCustomer number is %d", customer);
    printf("\nNumber of weeks rent due is %d", weeks);
    printf("\nRent per week is %.2f", rent);
    printf("\n\nRental due is %.2f\n\n", due);
}
```

Running this program gives:

```
Enter customer number 3333
Enter number of weeks rent due 2
Enter type of rental - c for Colour TV
                       b for Black and white TV
                       v for Video
                       o for other b


TV RENTAL BILL

Customer number is 3333
Number of weeks rent due is 2
Rent per week is 1.75

Rental due is 3.50

Is there another bill to be processed (y or n)? y

Enter customer number 5555
Enter number of weeks rent due 1
Enter type of rental - c for Colour TV
                       b for Black and white TV
                       v for Video
                       o for other c


TV RENTAL BILL

Customer number is 5555
Number of weeks rent due is 1
Rent per week is 3.60
```

Rental due is 3.60

Is there another bill to be processed (y or n)? **y**

Enter customer number **7000**
Enter number of weeks rent due **1**
Enter type of rental - c for Colour TV
b for Black and white TV
v for Video
o for other **c**

TV RENTAL BILL

Customer number is 7000
Number of weeks rent due is 1
Rent per week is 3.60

Rental due is 3.60

Is there another bill to be processed (y or n)? **n**

4.5 Exiting From Loops

If a program is well structured there should be **no** reason to exit from the middle of a loop. However, in exceptional circumstances **break** and **exit()** may be used.

break

break sends control to the statement following the end of the loop. For example,

```
while (another_line > 0)
{
        .
        .
    another_line = another_line + 2;
    if (another_line == 66)
        break;
        .
```

```
        .
}
page =
        .
        .
        .
```

If the **break** statement is executed the next statement obeyed is

```
page =
```

exit()

exit() not only leaves the loop but the whole program. Hence program control will be returned to the operating system. For example,

```
while (another_line>0)
{
        .
        .
    another_line = another_line+2;
    if (another_line == 66)
    exit();
        .
        .
}
page =
        .
        .
```

If **exit()** is executed the rest of the program is ignored and control returns to the operating system.

4.6 Programming Exercises

1. Write a program that will input a number and print out that number of *Hello there* s.

2. Write a program to produce a table for converting temperatures in degrees Celsius to degrees Fahrenheit. The table should have entries for 0 to 30 degrees Celsius. (NB C = (5/9)*(F-32))

3. Write a function power(x,n) which returns the value of x raised to the power of n.

Write a program to test your function which inputs pairs of values for x and n and prints the value of x to the power of n. (NB Don't forget the special cases of powers 0 and 1).

5 Pointers

Before extending the TV Rental Program we will sort out one of the programming restrictions imposed earlier, which limited our ability to produce a well-structured program. This is due to having to include the customer_input section in main() rather than in a function of its own. Until now our use of functions has been limited by only being able to return one variable to the calling function. The customer_input section requires the values of two to be returned.

Also, until now it has only been possible to use the input function scanf() in the main() section of the program.

Both these restrictions can be overcome by using **pointers**.

5.1 Pointers And scanf()

In the scanf() statement each variable name is preceded by an &. This indicates that we are referring to the **address** (or **location**) of the variable, rather than to the variable itself. In other words the variable list is a **list of pointers** indicating where the inputs are to be put.

For example

&no_1 is a pointer to the address (location) of the variable no_1

In the majority of cases the variable list in a scanf() statement will consist of only one variable. This is to allow a prompt to be output, using **printf()**, indicating the particular input required.

5.2 Pointers And Functions

Consider the print_bill() function from the TV Rental Program. The function heading is

```
print_bill(customer, weeks, rent, due)
int customer, weeks;
float rent, due;
```

which in essence sets up four variables **local** to the function print_bill, called

customer, weeks, rent and due.

The call from main() to the function is

```
print_bill(customer_no, no_of_weeks, rent_per_week, bill);
```

This passes the **values** contained in its variable list to its respective local variable in the function call. That is, if customer_no has a value of 1234 then the variable customer is given the value 1234. Note that it is the **value** that is passed, not the variables location.

However, if we were to pass the **address (location)** of a variable to a function, then its **value** could be accessed/changed in the body of the function. We already know how to indicate an address (location) of a variable as opposed to its value (i.e. put an & in front of the variable name).

As the address (location) of a variable is passed to the function then this variable is just updated in the function rather than having to pass a value back to the calling function. Hence the values of more than one variable can be changed from a function.

Consider the TV Rental Program, in particular main(). We are now going to move the program inputs into a function of their own called customer_input().

The call to this function would be

```
customer_input(&customer_no, &no_of_weeks);
```

This assumes that the function will input two values and put them into the variables customer_no and no_of_weeks.

With this change main() will now be

```
main()
{
   int no_of_weeks, customer_no;
   float rent_per_week, bill, weeks_rental(), calc_bill();
   char another_bill;

   /*Produce required number of bills*/
   do
     {
    /*Input customers details*/
    customer_input(&customer_no, &no_of_weeks);

     /*Determine rent per week - colour TV is 3.60*/
```

```
        rent_per_week = weeks_rental();

        /*Calculate and print bill for acceptable TV types*/
        if (rent_per_week != 0)
        {
          /*Calculate bill*/
          bill = calc_bill(no_of_weeks, rent_per_week);

          /*Print the bill*/
          print_bill(customer_no, no_of_weeks, rent_per_week, bill);
        }

        /*Another bill*/
        printf("Is there another bill to be processed (y or n)? ");
        scanf("%s",&another_bill);
        }
        while(another_bill == 'y');
}
```

In other words our main() function solely consists of control statements and function calls contributing to a well structured program.

Now to write the function customer_input().

```
customer_input(customer, weeks)     /*Input customer information*/
int *customer, *weeks;
{
    /*Input customer number and number of weeks rent due*/
    printf("\nEnter customer number ");
    scanf("%4d",customer);
    printf("Enter number of weeks rent due ");
    scanf("%2d",weeks);
}
```

There are two points to note in this function. Firstly, in the parameter definition

```
customer_input(customer, weeks)
int *customer, *weeks;
```

The * is used to indicate that customer and weeks are **pointers** to two variables of type **int**.

The call in main() to this function

```
customer_input(&customer_no, &no_of_weeks);
```

means that customer is **pointing** to the **address** of customer_no and weeks is pointing to the address of no_of_weeks.

Note that & is not put in front of the variable in the scanf() function. This is because customer and weeks are already pointers to the address of variables.

Making these changes to the TV Rental Program gives

```
#include <stdio.h>

/* TV RENTAL BILLS - Version 10
  - Production of an UNSPECIFIED number of
    bills for those renting colour and
    black and white TV s and videos
  - Creation of a function to handle inputs*/

main()
{
    int no_of_weeks, customer_no;
    float rent_per_week, bill, weeks_rental(), calc_bill();
    char another_bill;

    /*Produce required number of bills*/
    do
      {
     /*Input customers details*/
     customer_input(&customer_no, &no_of_weeks);

      /*Determine rent per week - colour TV is 3.60*/
      rent_per_week = weeks_rental();

      /*Calculate and print bill for acceptable TV types*/
      if (rent_per_week != 0)
      {
        /*Calculate bill*/
        bill = calc_bill(no_of_weeks, rent_per_week);

        /*Print the bill*/
        print_bill(customer_no, no_of_weeks, rent_per_week, bill);
      }

      /*Another bill*/
      printf("Is there another bill to be processed (y or n)? ");
      scanf("%s",&another_bill);
      }
```

```
    while(another_bill = = 'y');
}

customer_input(customer, weeks)     /*Input customer information*/
int *customer, *weeks;
{
    /*Input customer number and number of weeks rent due*/
    printf("\nEnter customer number ");
    scanf("%4d",customer);
    printf("Enter number of weeks rent due ");
    scanf("%2d",weeks);
}

float weeks_rental()   /*Determine rent per week*/
{
    char tv_type;

    /*Input TV type*/
    printf("Enter type of rental - c for Colour TV");
    printf("\n                      b for Black and white TV");
    printf("\n                      v for Video");
    printf("\n                      o for other ");
    scanf("%s",&tv_type);

    /*Determine rent per week*/
    switch (tv_type)
    {
    case 'c': /*Colour TV rental is 3.60*/
        return(3.60);
    case 'b': /*Black and white TV rental is 1.75*/
        return(1.75);
    case 'v': /*Video rental is 1.50*/
        return(1.50);
    default : /*Illegal input for tv_type*/
        printf("\nProgram does not handle this type of rental\n");
        return(0);
    }
}

float calc_bill(weeks, rent)   /*Calculate customers bill)*/
int weeks;
float rent;
{
    return(weeks * rent);
```

```
}

print_bill(customer, weeks, rent, due)  /*Calculate and print the bill*/
int customer, weeks;
float rent, due;
{
    printf("\n\nTV RENTAL BILL");
    printf("\n\nCustomer number is %d", customer);
    printf("\nNumber of weeks rent due is %d", weeks);
    printf("\nRent per week is %.2f", rent);
    printf("\n\nRental due is %.2f\n\n", due);
}
```

Running this program gives:

```
Enter customer number 1234
Enter number of weeks rent due 2
Enter type of rental - c for Colour TV
                       b for Black and white TV
                       v for Video
                       o for other b


TV RENTAL BILL

Customer number is 1234
Number of weeks rent due is 2
Rent per week is 1.75

Rental due is 3.50

Is there another bill to be processed (y or n)? y

Enter customer number 2323
Enter number of weeks rent due 1
Enter type of rental - c for Colour TV
                       b for Black and white TV
                       v for Video
                       o for other c


TV RENTAL BILL

Customer number is 2323
```

Number of weeks rent due is 1
Rent per week is 3.60

Rental due is 3.60

Is there another bill to be processed (y or n)? **n**

Another example of the use of pointers can be seen in the following function swap() which is passed two values and swaps them around (i.e. no_1 takes the value of no_2 and no_2 takes the value of no_1).

```
swap(no_1,no_2)
int *no_1,*no_2;
{
    int temp;
    temp = *no_1;
    *no_1 = *no_2;
    *no_2 = temp;
}
```

Note that in the function body we always have to use the pointer to the variables to indicate the contents of the location (e.g. no_1 is the address (location) and *no_1 indicates the content).

Returning to our TV Rental Program, currently input is performed in two places, customer_input and weeks _rental(). Altering the program so that all the inputs, more logically, occur in the customer_input function gives

```
#include <stdio.h>

    /* TV RENTAL BILLS - Version 11
   - Production of an UNSPECIFIED number of
    bills for those renting colour and
    black and white TV s and videos
   - Moving ALL the inputs (including tv type)into the SAME function*/

main()
    {
    int no_of_weeks, customer_no;
    float rent_per_week, bill, weeks_rental(), calc_bill();
    char another_bill, tv_type;

    /*Produce required number of bills*/
    do
      {
```

```
            /*Input customers details*/
            customer_input(&customer_no, &no_of_weeks, &tv_type);

            /*Determine rent per week - colour TV is 3.60*/
            rent_per_week = weeks_rental(tv_type);

            /*Calculate and print bill for acceptable TV types*/
            if (rent_per_week != 0)
            {
                /*Calculate bill*/
                bill = calc_bill(no_of_weeks, rent_per_week);

                /*Print the bill*/
                print_bill(customer_no, no_of_weeks, rent_per_week, bill);
            }

            /*Another bill*/
            printf("Is there another bill to be processed (y or n)? ");
            scanf("%s",&another_bill);
        }
        while(another_bill == 'y');
}

customer_input(customer, weeks, type)    /*Input customer information*/
int *customer, *weeks;
char *type;
{
    /*Input customer number and number of weeks rent due*/
    printf("\nEnter customer number ");
    scanf("%4d",customer);
    printf("Enter number of weeks rent due ");
    scanf("%2d",weeks);

    /*Input TV type*/
    printf("Enter type of rental - c for Colour TV");
    printf("\n                        b for Black and white TV");
    printf("\n                        v for Video");
    printf("\n                        o for other ");
    scanf("%s",type);
}

float weeks_rental(type)  /*Determine rent per week*/
char type;
```

```
{
    /*Determine rent per week*/
    switch (type)
    {
    case 'c': /*Colour TV rental is 3.60*/
            return(3.60);
    case 'b': /*Black and white TV rental is 1.75*/
            return(1.75);
    case 'v': /*Video rental is 1.50*/
            return(1.50);
    default : /*Illegal input for tv_type*/
            printf("\nProgram does not handle this type of rental\n");
            return(0);
    }
}

float calc_bill(weeks, rent)    /*Calculate customers bill)*/
int weeks;
float rent;
{
    return(weeks * rent);
}

print_bill(customer, weeks, rent, due)  /*Calculate and print the bill*/
int customer, weeks;
float rent, due;
    {
    printf("\n\nTV RENTAL BILL");
    printf("\n\nCustomer number is %d", customer);
    printf("\nNumber of weeks rent due is %d", weeks);
    printf("\nRent per week is %.2f", rent);
    printf("\n\nRental due is %.2f\n\n", due);
}
```

Running this program gives:

Enter customer number **1234**
Enter number of weeks rent due **10**
Enter type of rental - c for Colour TV
                       b for Black and white TV
                       v for Video
                       o for other **b**

TV RENTAL BILL

Customer number is 1234
Number of weeks rent due is 10
Rent per week is 1.75

Rental due is 17.50

Is there another bill to be processed (y or n)? **y**

Enter customer number **7777**
Enter number of weeks rent due **2**
Enter type of rental - c for Colour TV
b for Black and white TV
v for Video
o for other **c**

TV RENTAL BILL

Customer number is 7777
Number of weeks rent due is 2
Rent per week s 3.60

Rental due is 7.20

Is there another bill to be processed (y or n)? **n**

5.3 Programming Exercises

1. Write a function order() which is passed two numbers and arranges them in ascending order.
   Test your function by writing a program to input a number of pairs of numbers. Each pair of numbers will then be output in ascending order.

2. A dressmaking shop sells material in yards, feet and inches. However, patterns give the material requirements in metres.
   Write a program to aid sales staff that converts material requirements in metres to yards, feet and inches.

3. A company employs staff on both a weekly salary and on an hourly rate. At the end of each week a payroll run is done which produces:

- a payslip for each employee
- a breakdown of the currency denominations required to make up each pay packet.

Write a program to meet payroll needs of this company. For each employee input to the program will be:

- employee number
- indication as to whether employee hourly or weekly paid
- weeks salary or rate of pay per hour
- number of hours worked for those on hourly rates.

NB This is a very simplified payroll and takes no account of tax, insurance, overtime, etc. Rounding errors may occur.

6 Simple Arrays

The TV Rental Program currently produces bills for a number of customers. From the company's point of view it would be useful if the program produced a summary report of all the bills produced in one run.

In order to do this all the information computed for each bill must be stored in the program and then output in the form of a summary table after the last bill has been produced.

Currently once a bill has been output, its information is overwritten by the information input for the next customer.

For example, the information that would need to be kept in order to provide a summary report is laid out in tabular form below.

Customer number	*No. of weeks*	*Rental Type*	*Rent Due*
23	1	c	3.60
7	3	b	5.25
1	2	v	3.00
9	1	v	1.50
28	1	c	3.60
46	2	c	7.20

A convenient method of keeping this information would be for the program to store four tables -

1. Customer number
2. No of weeks
3. Rental type
4. Rent due

In order to set up these tables it is necessary to declare them much in the same way as variables have been declared but giving some indication of the number of entries that there will be in the table. For example customer number would be declared as

```
int customer_no[50];
```

This sets up a table called customer_no in which each entry is an integer. The [50] indicates that the table is set up with 50 entries, which are referred to as 0, 1, 2, 3 ...... 49.

In computer terms such a table is known as an **array** and each entry in the array as an **array element.**

It is possible to access particular array elements. For example the fourth element in the array customer_no would be

```
customer_no[3]
```

(NB remember the first element of the array is the '0' th element.)

Using an **array index,** for example called i, then the i th **element** is referred to as

```
customer_no[i]
```

Obviously, i is a variable of type **int.**

Returning to the TV Rental Program, in order to keep information on up to 50 customers we would need to change the variables required in our table to arrays. That is

```
int no_of_weeks[50], customer_no[50], i;
char another_bill, tv_type[50];
```

Other changes have to be made to the existing TV Rental Program to allow use to be made of these arrays. Everywhere one of the variables in the table is used we must specify the particular element of the array that is being referred to. This is done by initialising the element index at the start of the program and increasing it every time a set of customer information is input. Hence before the loop include the instruction

```
i=0;
```

then increment the index everytime the loop is entered by

```
++i;
```

All that then has to be done is to insert [i] next to every array element.

These changes to the main() function can be seen in the TV Rental Program below. The other functions do not require changing as we are still passing or returning single variables rather than complete tables.

Note that one other small change has to be made to the loop in the main() function. Currently it is repeated until there are no more customer bills. However, if there are more than 50 bills then there will be no space in the arrays to store them, in which case the program will fail. Hence the **while** statement should be changed to

```
while(another_bill = = 'y' && i < = 50);
```

```
#include <stdio.h>

/* TV RENTAL BILLS - Version 12
 - Storing the customer information for a
   maximum of 50 customers using arrays*/

main()
{
    int no_of_weeks[50], customer_no[50], i;
    float rent_per_week, bill, weeks_rental(), calc_bill();
    char another_bill, tv_type[50];

    i = 0;

    /*Produce required number of bills*/
    do
    {
        /*Add 1 to the array index*/
        + +i;

        /*Input customers details*/
        customer_input(&customer_no[i], &no_of_weeks[i], &tv_type[i]);

        /*Determine rent per week - colour TV is 3.60*/
        rent_per_week = weeks_rental(tv_type[i]);

        /*Calculate and print bill for acceptable TV types*/
        if (rent_per_week ! = 0)
        {
            /*Calculate bill*/
            bill = calc_bill(no_of_weeks[i], rent_per_week);

            /*Print the bill*/
            print_bill(customer_no[i], no_of_weeks[i], rent_per_week, bill);
        }

        /*Another bill*/
        printf("Is there another bill to be processed (y or n)? ");
        scanf("%s",&another_bill);
    }
```

```
        while(another_bill = = 'y' && i < = 50);
}

customer_input(customer, weeks, type)    /*Input customer information*/
int *customer, *weeks;
char *type;
   {
   /*Input customer number and number of weeks rent due*/
   printf("\nEnter customer number ");
   scanf("%4d",customer);
   printf("Enter number of weeks rent due ");
   scanf("%2d",weeks);

   /*Input TV type*/
   printf("Enter type of rental - c for Colour TV");
   printf("\n                      b for Black and white TV");
   printf("\n                      v for Video");
   printf("\n                      o for other ");
   scanf("%s",type);
}

float weeks_rental(type)   /*Determine rent per week*/
char type;
{
   /*Determine rent per week*/
   switch (type)
   {
   case 'c': /*Colour TV rental is 3.60*/
         return(3.60);
   case 'b': /*Black and white TV rental is 1.75*/
         return(1.75);
   case 'v': /*Video rental is 1.50*/
         return(1.50);
   default : /*Illegal input for tv_type*/
         printf("\nProgram does not handle this type of rental\n");
         return(0);
   }
}

float calc_bill(weeks, rent)    /*Calculate customers bill)*/
int weeks;
float rent;
{
   return(weeks * rent);
```

```
}

print_bill(customer, weeks, rent, due)  /*Calculate and print the bill*/
int customer, weeks;
float rent, due;
{
    printf("\n\nTV RENTAL BILL");
    printf("\n\nCustomer number is %d", customer);
    printf("\nNumber of weeks rent due is %d", weeks);
    printf("\nRent per week is %.2f", rent);
    printf("\n\nRental due is %.2f\n\n", due);
}
```

Running this program gives:

```
Enter customer number 1111
Enter number of weeks rent due 2
Enter type of rental - c for Colour TV
                       b for Black and white TV
                       v for Video
                       o for other c


TV RENTAL BILL

Customer number is 1111
Number of weeks rent due is 2
Rent per week is 3.60

Rental due is 7.20

Is there another bill to be processed (y or n)? y

Enter customer number 44
Enter number of weeks rent due 1
Enter type of rental - c for Colour TV
                       b for Black and white TV
                       v for Video
                       o for other v


TV RENTAL BILL

Customer number is 44
```

```
Number of weeks rent due is 1
Rent per week is 1.50

Rental due is 1.50

Is there another bill to be processed (y or n)? n
```

The TV Rental Program is now storing all the information needed to produce a summary report except for the rent due, which is calculated and held in the **variable** bill. Hence the **variable** bill has to be turned into an **array**. This requires the declaration in main() to be changed and the reference to bill to be indexed.

Making thesechanges to the TV Rental Program gives

```
#include <stdio.h>

/* TV RENTAL BILLS - Version 13
  - Storing the customer information and bill for
    a maximum of 50 customers using arrays*/

main()
{
    int no_of_weeks[50], customer_no[50], i;
    float rent_per_week, bill[50], weeks_rental(), calc_bill();
    char another_bill, tv_type[50];

    i = 0;

    /*Produce required number of bills*/
    do
      {
      /*Add 1 to the array index*/
       + +i;

     /*Input customers details*/
     customer_input(&customer_no[i], &no_of_weeks[i], &tv_type[i]);

      /*Determine rent per week - colour TV is 3.60*/
      rent_per_week = weeks_rental(tv_type[i]);

      /*Calculate and print bill for acceptable TV types*/
      if (rent_per_week != 0)
      {
        /*Calculate bill*/
```

```
            bill[i] = calc_bill(no_of_weeks[i], rent_per_week);

            /*Print the bill*/
            print_bill(customer_no[i], no_of_weeks[i], rent_per_week, bill[i]);
          }

        /*Another bill*/
        printf("Is there another bill to be processed (y or n)? ");
        scanf("%s",&another_bill);
        }
        while(another_bill = = 'y' && i < = 50);
}

customer_input(customer, weeks, type)    /*Input customer information*/
int *customer, *weeks;
char *type;
{
    /*Input customer number and number of weeks ent due*/
    printf("\nEnter customer number ");
    scanf("%4d",customer);
    printf("Enter number of weeks rent due ");
    scanf("%2d",weeks);

    /*Input TV type*/
    printf("Enter type of rental - c for Colour TV");
    printf("\n                     b for Black and white TV");
    printf("\n                     v for Video");
    printf("\n                     o for other ");
    scanf("%s",type);
}

float weeks_rental(type)   /*Determine rent per week*/
char type;
{
    /*Determine rent per week*/
    switch (type)
    {
    case 'c': /*Colour TV rental is 3.60*/
          return(3.60);
    case 'b': /*Black and white TV rental is 1.75*/
          return(1.75);
    case 'v': /*Video rental is 1.50*/
          return(1.50);
    default : /*Illegal input for tv_type*/
```

```
        printf("\nProgram does not handle this type of rental\n");
        return(0);
    }
}

float calc_bill(weeks, rent)   /*Calculate customers bill)*/
int weeks;
float rent;
{
    return(weeks * rent);
}

print_bill(customer, weeks, rent, due)  /*Calculate and print the bill*/
int customer, weeks;
float rent, due;
{
    printf("\n\nTV RENTAL BILL");
    printf("\n\nCustomer number is %d", customer);
    printf("\nNumber of weeks rent due is %d", weeks);
    printf("\nRent per week is %.2f", rent);
    printf("\n\nRental due is %.2f\n\n", due);
}
```

Running this program gives:

Enter customer number **12**
Enter number of weeks rent due **3**
Enter type of rental - c for Colour TV
b for Black and white TV
v for Video
o for other **c**

TV RENTAL BILL

Customer number is 12
Number of weeks rent due is 3
Rent per week is 3.60

Rental due is 10.80

Is there another bill to be processed (y or n)? **y**

Enter customer number **123**

```
Enter number of weeks rent due 2
Enter type of rental - c for Colour TV
                       b for Black and white TV
                       v for Video
                       o for other b


TV RENTAL BILL

Customer number is 123
Number of weeks rent due is 2
Rent per week is 1.75

Rental due is 3.50

Is there another bill to be processed (y or n)? n
```

Now that all the information is being stored a new function summary() can be added which produces a summary report. This will be called from main() once all the customer bills have been produced. In this call we will be passing **complete arrays** to the function. This is done by passing the array name rather than a particular element. Hence as **array name** is treated as the **address of the array** the call will be

```
summary(customer_no, no_of_weeks, tv_type, bill, i);
```

where i is the number of bills produced and therefore the number of entries in the summary table. The function definition will be

```
summary(customer, weeks, type, due, no_of_customers)
int *customer, *weeks, no_of_customers;
char *type;
float *due;
```

When referring to an element of an array inside a function we use the same syntax as in main(), i.e. the * is not required. For example, the third customer will be customer[3].

For the same reason the & is required before the array element in a scanf() function. For example,

```
scanf("%d", &customer[3]);
```

The TV Rental Program, including a summary function to produce a table of the form,

```
Customer number   Weeks due   Rental type   Rent due
       .              .            .            .
       .              .            .            .
       .              .            .            .
       .              .            .            .
       .              .            .            .
                                           ----------
                                   Total
                                           ----------
```

is as follows

```
#include < stdio.h >

/* TV RENTAL BILLS - Version 14
 - A summary table is produced once all the
   customer bills have been output*/

main()
{
    int no_of_weeks[50], customer_no[50], i;
    float rent_per_week, bill[50], weeks_rental(), calc_bill();
    char another_bill, tv_type[50];

    i = 0;

    /*Produce required number of bills*/
    do
    {
        /*Add 1 to the array index*/
        + +i;

        /*Input customers details*/
        customer_input(&customer_no[i], &no_of_weeks[i], &tv_type[i]);

        /*Determine rent per week - colour TV is 3.60*/
        rent_per_week = weeks_rental(tv_type[i]);

        /*Calculate and print bill for acceptable TV types*/
        if (rent_per_week ! = 0)
        {
            /*Calculate bill*/
            bill[i] = calc_bill(no_of_weeks[i], rent_per_week);
```

```
            /*Print the bill*/
            print_bill(customer_no[i], no_of_weeks[i], rent_per_week, bill[i]);
        }

        /*Another bill*/
        printf("Is there another bill to be processed (y or n)? ");
        scanf("%s",&another_bill);
    }
    while(another_bill = = 'y' && i < = 50);

    /*Print summary table*/
    summary(customer_no, no_of_weeks, tv_type, bill, i);
}

customer_input(customer, weeks, type)    /*Input customer information*/
int *customer, *weeks;
char *type;
{
    /*Input customer number and number of weeks rent due*/
    printf("\nEnter customer number ");
    scanf("%4d",customer);
    printf("Enter number ofweeks rent due ");
    scanf("%2d",weeks);

    /*Input TV type*/
    printf("Enter type of rental - c for Colour TV");
    printf("\n                  b for Black and white TV");
    printf("\n                  v for Video");
    printf("\n                  o for other ");
    scanf("%s",type);
}

float weeks_rental(type)  /*Determine rent per week*/
char type;
{
    /*Determine rent per week*/
    switch (type)
    {
    case 'c': /*Colour TV rental is 3.60*/
        return(3.60);
    case 'b': /*Black and white TV rental is 1.75*/
        return(1.75);
    case 'v': /*Video rental is 1.50*/
        return(1.50);
```

```
    default : /*Illegal input for tv_type*/
        printf("\nProgram does not handle this type of rental\n");
        return(0);
    }
}

float calc_bill(weeks, rent)   /*Calculate customers bill)*/
int weeks;
float rent;
{
    return(weeks * rent);
}

print_bill(customer, weeks, rent, due) /*Calculate and print the bill*/
int customer, weeks;
float rent, due;
{
    printf("\n\nTV RENTAL BILL");
    printf("\n\nCustomer number is %d", customer);
    printf("\nNumber of weeks rent due is %d", weeks);
    printf("\nRent per week is %.2f", rent);
    printf("\n\nRental due is %.2f\n\n", due);
}

summary(customer, weeks, type, due, no_of_customers) /*Produce summary report*/
int *customer, *weeks, no_of_customers;
char *type;
float *due;
{
    int i;  /*loop control variable*/
    float total;
    total = 0;    /*Initialise total*/

    /*Print table headings*/
    printf("\n\n              SUMMARY REPORT");
    printf("\n              --------------");
    printf("\n\nCustomer number  Weeks due  Rental type  Rent due");
    printf("\n---------------  ---------  -----------  --------");

    /*Print table of customer information*/
    for (i = 1; i < = no_of_customers; i+ + )
        printf("\n    %4d          %2d          %c       %6.2f",
                                customer[i], weeks[i], type[i], due[i]);
```

```
    /*Calculate total rent due*/
    for (i = 1; i < = no_of_customers; i+ + )
        total = total + due[i];

    /*Print total rent due*/
    printf("\n\n                Total rent due is %12.2f\n\n", total);
}
```

Running this program gives:

```
Enter customer number 1111
Enter number of weeks rent due 2
Enter type of rental - c for Colour TV
                       b for Black and white TV
                       v for Video
                       o for other c


TV RENTAL BILL

Customer number is 1111
Number of weeks rent due is 2
Rent per week is 3.60

Rental due is 7.20

Is there another bill to be processed (y or n)? y

Enter customer number 2222
Enter number of weeks rent due 3
Enter type of rental - c for Colour TV
                       b for Black and white TV
                       v for Video
                       o for other b


TV RENTAL BILL

Customer number is 2222
Number of weeks rent due is 3
Rent per week is 1.75

Rental due is 5.25
```

```
Is there another bill to be processed (y or n)? y

Enter customer number 3333
Enter number of weeks rent due 10
Enter type of rental - c for Colour TV
                      b for Black and white TV
                      v for Video
                      o for other c


TV RENTAL BILL

Customer number is 3333
Number of weeks rent due is 10
Rent per week is 3.60

Rental due is 36.00

Is there another bill to be processed (y or n)? n


SUMMARY REPORT
------------------------------

Customer number  Weeks due  Rental type  Rent due
---------------  ---------  -----------  --------
     1111            2           c         7.20
     2222            3           b         5.25
     3333           10           c        36.00

        Total rent due is                 48.45
```

6.1 Programming Exercises

1. Write a program to input a series of numbers. This list should then be output together with the average value of the series.

2. Write a program to input a name, consisting of christian name followed by surname (NB separated with a space), and store it as a string of characters in an array of type char.

   The program will then output

   - the name

- the name such that the surname is output first.

Hint: Use getchar() to input a string of characters. getchar() inputs one character at a time when the input buffer is flushed using the return character.

3. If string is an array containing a string of characters (mixed upper and lower case), write the following functions

- lowercase(string) which converts all the characters in the string to lower case, using the built-in function tolower(c).
- capital(string) which converts all characters in the string to capital letters using the built in function toupper(c).
- reverse(string) which reverses the order of the characters in the string.

Write a program to read in a string of characters and output the string in lower case, capital letters and reverse order.

7 Structures

Returning to the TV Rental Program, consider the calls to the functions, customer_input() and print_bill():

```
customer_input(&customer_no[i], &no_of_weeks[i], &tv_type[i]);

print_bill(customer_no[i], no_of_weeks[i], rent_per_week, bill[i]);
```

In each case the parameter list is starting to become unwieldy. Also, in all the function calls we are passing/returning almost identical information about one customer. It would be convenient if all the information about the customer could be grouped together, with one name assigned to it. This group name could then be passed to the functions.

In C this can be done using **structures**. For example, we can define a structure called customer_record that will contain all the information relevant to one customer. That is

```
struct customer_record        /*Defining a customer record*/
    {
    int customer_no;
    int no_of_weeks;
    char tv_type;
    float bill;
    };
```

A variable called customer which is of type customer_record can now be declared by

```
struct customer_record customer;
```

A variable can also be declared by inserting it before the last ; in the structure definition. For example,

```
struct customer_record        /*Defining a customer record*/
    {
    int customer_no;
    int no_of_weeks;
```

```
char tv_type;
float bill;
} customer;
```

It should now be obvious that all we are doing with structures is defining new variable types consisting of existing types. Hence the general syntax for defining structures is

```
struct structure_name
    {
        type variable_name;
        type variable_name;
    } structure_variable(s);
```

Any variable within the structure can be referred to by

```
structure_variable.variable_name
```

For example, customer is a structure of type customer_record so tv_type is now referred to as

```
customer_type
```

7.1 Passing Structures To Functions

Structure variables are passed to functions by passing the address of the start of the structure variable)i.e. its name . For example

```
customer_input(&customer);
```

The function parameter definition will now be

```
customer_input(cust)
struct customer_record *cust;
```

This is telling the program that cust is a pointer containing the address of the start of a variable which is a structure of type customer_record. Hence we are assuming that the function customer_input knows about the structure customer_record. Is this so?

If our program is of the form

```
*include <stdio.h>
  /*            */
  main()
  {
     structure_definition
  }
  function_1()
  {
        .
        .
  }
  function_2()
  {
        .
        .
  }
```

then as the structure is defined in main() it is only known to main() and can therefore only be used within main(). (i.e. it is local to its function). In order that a structure definition can be used throughout a program its definition must be global. This is done by putting the structure definition before main() (i.e. outside any function), giving

```
*include <stdio.h>
  /*            */
  structure_definition
  main()
  {
        .
        .
  }
  function_1()
  {
        .
        .
  }
  function_2()
  {
        .
        .
  }
```

Note, however, that declaring a variable of type structure is still done within the appropriate function.

Having established that a structure can be passed to a function, we must now consider how the individual elements of that structure can be referenced. This is done by using the pointer to the start of the structure and combining it with the element name. For example, with the function parameter definition

```
customer_input(cust)
    struct customer_record *cust;
```

the element tv_type will be referred to as

```
(*cust).tv_type
```

Note the brackets must be included as . is a higher priority operator than *. However, in C, the symbol - can also be used giving

```
cust-tv_type
```

Use whichever notation you are most happy with. After all the only difference between these versions is two characters. In this book the first of these notations will be used.

7.2 Structures And scanf()

Using scanf() it is possible to input information to a structure variable passed via function call. In this case a structure variable was passed to the function customer_input. Within this function scanf() is used to input information. If we use the structure definition customer_record defined at the beginning of this chapter, then the customer_input() function becomes

```
customer_input(cust)
    struct customer_record *cust;
    {
        /*Input customer number and number of weeks rent due*/
        printf("\nEnter customer number ");
        scanf("%4d", & (*cust).customer_no);
                .    .    .    .    .
                .    .    .    .    .
                .    .    .    .    .
```

7.3 TV Rental Program

The TV Rental Program has been altered to use structures. However, as consideration has not been given to arrays of structures yet, /* and */ have been put around the call to the function summary and the function itself has been removed. By doing this we are effectively reducing these parts of the program to comments, which will be skipped over on processing (NB comments cannot be nested).

```
#include <stdio.h>

/* TV RENTAL BILLS - Version 15
- Using structures*/

struct customer_record        /*Defining a customer record*/
    {
    int customer_no;
    int no_of_weeks;
    char tv_type;
    float bill;
    };

main()
{
    struct customer_record customer;
    float rent_per_week, weeks_rental(), calc_bill();
    char another_bill;

    /*Produce required number of bills*/
    do
    {
        /*Input customers details*/
        customer_input(&customer);

        /*Determine rent per week - colour TV is 3.60*/
        rent_per_week = weeks_rental(&customer);

        /*Calculate and print bill for acceptable TV types*/
        if (rent_per_week != 0)
        {
            /*Calculate bill*/
            customer.bill = calc_bill(&customer, rent_per_week);
```

```
        /*Print the bill*/
        print_bill(&customer, rent_per_week);
      }

      /*Another bill*/
      printf("Is there another bill to be processed (y or n)? ");
      scanf("%s",&another_bill);
      }
      while(another_bill = = 'y');

   /*Print summary table*/
   /*summary(customer_no, no_of_weeks, tv_type, bill, i);*/
}

customer_input(cust)    /*Input customer information*/
struct customer_record *cust
{
   /*Input customer number and number of weeks rent due*/
   printf("\nEnter customer number ");
   scanf("%4d", & (*cust).customer_no);
   printf("Enter number of weeks rent due ");
   scanf("%2d", & (*cust).no_of_weeks);

   /*Input TV type*/
   printf("Enter type of rental - c for Colour TV");
   printf("\n                  b for Black and white TV");
   printf("\n                  v for Video");
   printf("\n                  o for other ");
   scanf("%s", & (*cust).tv_type);
}

float weeks_rental(cust)  /*Determine rent per week*/
struct customer_record *cust;
{
   /*Determine rent per week*/
   switch ((*cust).tv_type)
   {
   case 'c': /*Colour TV rental is 3.60*/
         return(3.60);
   case 'b': /*Black and white TV rental is 1.75*/
         return(1.75);
   case 'v': /*Video rental is 1.50*/
         return(1.50);
   default : /*Illegal input for tv_type*/
```

```
        printf("\nProgram does not handle this type of rental\n");
        return(0);
    }
}

float calc_bill(cust, rent)    /*Calculate customers bill)*/
struct customer_record *cust;
float rent;
{
    return((*cust).no_of_weeks * rent);
}

print_bill(cust,rent)  /*Calculate and print the bill*/
struct customer_record *cust;
float rent;
{
    printf("\n\nTV RENTAL BILL");
    printf("\n\nCustomer number is %d", (*cust).customer_no);
    printf("\nNumber of weeks rent due is %d", (*cust).no_of_weeks);
    printf("\nRent per week is %.2f", rent);
    printf("\n\nRental due is %.2f\n\n", (*cust).bill);
}
```

Running this program gives:

```
Enter customer number 2222
Enter number of weeks rent due 4
Enter type of rental - c for Colour TV
                       b for Black and white TV
                       v for Video
                       o for other c


TV RENTAL BILL

Customer number is 2222
Number of weeks rent due is 4
Rent per week is 3.60

Rental due is 14.40

Is there another bill to be processed (y or n)? y

Enter customer number 4444
```

```
Enter number of weeks rent due 2
Enter type of rental - c for Colour TV
                       b for Black and white TV
                       v for Video
                       o for other b


TV RENTAL BILL

Customer number is 4444
Number of weeks rent due is 2
Rent per week is 1.75

Rental due is 3.50

Is there another bill to be processed (y or n)? n
```

7.4 Structures And Arrays

In order to produce the summary table in the TV Rental Program all the customer information was held in arrays. The program has been altered so that the information for one customer is now linked together as a structure. Therefore to hold all the information required for the summary table we must be able to define an array in which each element takes the form of the relevant structure. Assuming the structure customer_record has been defined we can declare an array called customer by

```
struct customer_record customer[50];
```

This gives us an array of 51 elements each of type customer_record.

Any element within this array is referred to by an **index**. For example tv_type for customer 3 will be

```
customer[3].tv_type
```

Using arrays of structures within functions

Firstly, within the TV Rental Program it is necessary to be able to pass information on an individual customer. This is done by including the index after the array name. For example

```
customer_input(&customer[i]);
```

The function definitions will remain the same as they were as only one customer is being dealt with at any time.

To produce the summary table we have to pass complete arrays to the function summary. The call to the function will be

```
summary(customer, i);
```

Remember with arrays, by passing its name we are passing the address of the start of the array.

Therefore the function definition is

```
summary(cust, no_of_customers)
    struct customer_record *cust;
    int no_of_customers;
```

If within our function we need to refer to a particular element then it is stated after the structure name, e.g. we wold refe to the ith element of the array as

```
*cust[i]
```

However, if we wish to refer to a particular part of the structure for this element then it would be

```
(*cust[i]).tv_type
```

The TV Rental Program shown below, as well as producing customer bills, also produces a summary table for a maximum of 50 customers.

```
#include <stdio.h>

/* TV RENTAL BILLS - Version 16
- Using arrays of structures*/

struct customer_record        /*Defining a customer record*/
{
int customer_no;
int no_of_weeks;
char tv_type;
float bill;
};
```

```
main()
{
    struct customer_record customer[50];
    float rent_per_week, weeks_rental(), calc_bill();
    char another_bill;
    int i;

    i = 0;

    /*Produce required number of bills*/
    do
    {
        /*Add 1 to the array index*/
        + +i;

        /*Input customers details*/
        customer_input(&customer[i]);

        /*Determine rent per week - colour TV is 3.60*/
        rent_per_week = weeks_rental(&customer[i]);

        /*Calculate and print bill for acceptable TV types*/
        if (rent_per_week ! = 0)
        {
            /*Calculate bill*/
            customer[i].bill = calc_bill(&customer[i], rent_per_week);

            /*Print the bill*/
            print_bill(&customer[i], rent_per_week);
        }

        /*Another bill*/
        printf("Is there another bill to be processed (y or n)? ");
        scanf("%s",&another_bill);
    }
    while(another_bill = = 'y' && i < = 50);

    /*Print summary table*/
    summary(customer, i);
}

customer_input(cust)    /*Input customer information*/
struct customer_record *cust;
{
```

```
    /*Input customer number and number of weeks rent due*/
    printf("\nEnter customer number ");
    scanf("%4d", & (*cust).customer_no);
    printf("Enter number of weeks rent due ");
    scanf("%2d", & (*cust).no_of_weeks);

    /*Input TV type*/
    printf("Enter type of rental - c for Colour TV");
    printf("\n                    b for Black and white TV");
    printf("\n                    v for Video");
    printf("\n                    o for other ");
    scanf("%s", & (*cust).tv_type);
}

float weeks_rental(cust)   /*Determine rent per week*/
struct customer_record *cust;
}
    /*Determine rent per week
    switch ((*cust).tv_type)
    {
    case 'c': /*Colour TV rental is 3.60*/
            return(3.60);
    case 'b': /*Black and white TV rental is 1.75*/
            return(1.75);
    case 'v': /*Video rental is 1.50*/
            return(1.50);
    default : /*Illegal input for tv_type*/
            printf("\nProgram does not handle this type of rental\n");
            return(0);
    }
}

float calc_bill(cust, rent)    /*Calculate customers bill)*/
struct customer_record *cust;
float rent;
{
    return((*cust).no_of_weeks * rent);
}

print_bill(cust,rent)  /*Calculate and print the bill*/
struct customer_record *cust;
float rent;
{
    printf("\n\nTV RENTAL BILL");
```

```
    printf("\n\nCustomer number is %d", (*cust).customer_no);
    printf("\nNumber of weeks rent due is %d", (*cust).no_of_weeks);
    printf("\nRent per week is %.2f", rent);
    printf("\n\nRental due is %.2f\n\n", (*cust).bill);
}
```

summary(cust, no_of_customers) /*Produce summary report*/
struct customer_record *cust;

```
int no_of_customers;
{
    int i;  /*loop control variable*/
    float total;
    total = 0;    /*Initialise total*/

    /*Print table headings*/
    printf("\n\n            SUMMARY REPORT");
    printf("\n              ---------------");
    printf("\n\nCustomer number  Weeks due  Rental type  Rent due");
    printf("\n--------------- ---------  -----------  --------");

    /*Print table of customer information*/
    for (i = 1; i <= no_of_customers; i++)
        printf("\n     %4d          %2d          %c        %6.2f",
            cust[i].customer_no, cust[i].no_of_weeks, cust[i].tv_type,
                                                          cust[i].bill);

    /*Calculate total rent due*/
    for (i = 1; i <= no_of_customers; i++)
        total = total + cust[i].bill;

    /*Print total rent due*/
    printf("\n\n             Total rent due is %12.2f\n\n", total);
}
```

Running this program gives:

Enter customer number **2222**
Enter number of weeks rent due **10**
Enter type of rental - c for Colour TV
                       b for Black and white TV
                       v for Video
                       o for other **c**

TV RENTAL BILL

Customer number is 2222
Number of weeks rent due is 10
Rent per week is 3.60

Rental due is 36.00

Is there another bill to be processed (y or n)? **y**

Enter customer number **6666**
Enter number of weeks rent due **2**
Enter type of rental - c for Colour TV
b for Black and white TV
v for Video
o for other **b**

TV RENTAL BILL

Customer number is 6666
Number of weeks rent due is 2
Rent per week is 1.75

Rental due is 3.50

Is there another bill to be processed (y or n)? **n**

SUMMARY REPORT

Customer number	Weeks due	Rental type	Rent due
2222	10	c	36.00
6666	2	b	3.50
Total rent due is			39.50

7.5 Programming Exercises

1. Write a program that keeps account of the number of goals scored by

particular football players. (Maximum of 100 players).

The program should utilise a structure for each player consisting of his:

- name
- team
- number of goals scored

Not only should the program input and store this information, it should also allow for the number of goals to be updated for any player before outputting an up-to-data table.

8 File Organisation

Until now all the data used in our programs has been held in the computer's memory. Every time a program is run the data has to be keyed in again. This is all right if different data is to be used every time the program is run, but in many applications (for example payroll, stock processing) the same basic information is used time and time again. In these applications it would be better if the basic information only had to be input once via the keyboard and held in some way so that it could then be read directly into the computer. If this was so then only the alterations to the basic information would need to be keyed in when updating the information being held. In the same way information in the application that changes every time the application is run can still be entered from the keyboard.

The main means of storing information that can be read directly into the computer is by entering it into a file which is held on disk. Whenever, the information is required the program reads the information from the disk rather than from the keyboard. As any disk can contain a number of files each **file** must be given a name. Secondly, information cannot be output to the file in a haphazard manner. The information has to be organised.

8.1 Records

Any file is made up of a number of **records**. For example, if a file is to be set up to hold information about books, then for **each** book there will be **one** record. Hence if information on a hundred books is to be put onto file, then there will be one hundred records in the file. In diagrammatic form a file could be represented as

Record 1	Record 2	Record 3

or, for example,

Book 1	Book 2	Book 3 ..... Book 100

Any program using this file must know where each record starts and finishes. One means of doing this is to write an end of record marker to the file as it is being set up. In the C programming language the character <return> (i.e. \n) can be used to denote the end of a record.

8.2 Data Items

Each record is broken down into a number of **data items**. That is

Record	Item 1	Item 2	Item 3	Item 4

For example, if the information to be kept about each book is title, author and ISBN classification then the record would be

Title	Author	ISBN

with the actual information in the record being, for example,

From here to there	Smith J	0-23956

Hence, title, author and ISBN are the **names** of the data items and From here to there, Smith J and 0-23956 are the **actual** data (information) held in the record.

Note that all similar records in a file must consist of the same data items, in the same order.

As in the case of the records it is necessary to have some means of knowing where each data item starts and finishes. Again data item separators have to be determined when the file is being set up. There are two different ways in which **item separators** can be incorporated into the records.

Specified length

When each piece of data is written to the record its length is specified. For example,

Title could be determined as having a length of 60 characters
Author as having 15 characters
ISBN classification as having 12 characters.

Therefore, if in every record 60 characters are written for Title, etc., then on reading the information back from the file 60 characters are read for Title, etc. This however means that if the required length of the data item is less than 60 characters it will be padded out with spaces. If longer, only the first 60 characters will be stored the rest will be ignored.

Note that the length of each of the data items are the same in all records in the file. This obviously leads to wasted space in some records.

Item separators

In this case the items are separated by some known character, for example, a comma or a space. In our example this would give a record layout of

From here to there,Smith J,0-23956

Obviously, a space would be unsuitable as the data itself contains spaces.

When the file is set up an item separator is written to the record between each data item. When the record is read it is done character by character looking for the item separator to indicate when a complete item has been read.

This method is obviously slower than using the specified length method of item separators. However, there is no space wasted in the file.

8.3 File Organisations

Having looked at the make up of individual records it is now necessary to consider how these records can be combined to form a file. There are four standard file organisations.

- **Serial** files where records are put one after the other with no thought given to their order. On accessing the file the order of records should also be unimportant. Therefore this method of file organisation is usually used when all the records are required.
  For example, programs are held in serial files.
- **Sequential** files where records are processed serially, but they have been stored in the file in some pre-determined order.
  For example, payroll, personnel and stock files where the records

are used in the order in which they are held in the file (NB not all the records have to be used, it is the order that is important).

- **Indexed sequential** files contain the records in any order (like a serial file), however they are associated with an ordered index which points to the specific record. The advantage of this method of file organisation is that if the records are long (i.e. contain a lot of information) then the actual records do not have to be moved about. When new records are added they go at the end of the file. Only the index needs to be kept in order.
- **Random** files are used when records are likely to be accessed randomly. A typical example would be to request a listing of all books by SMITH J.
  Obviously, there has to be some method of knowing where individual records are. This is done by setting up the file using one of several address generation techniques.

8.4 Sequential File Organisation

In this book we will only be using sequential file organisations in which the records are ordered on either an alphabetic or numeric **key**.

For example, our file of book information could be ordered alphabetically by author or numerically by ISBN classification. It does not matter which, but once the file has been set up using a particular key field then that key field is used in all further processing.

Setting Up A Sequential File

The obvious way to set up a sequential file would be to order the records before putting them into the file. This is, however, prone to mistakes being made. The standard method of setting up a file in order to reduce errors is a two stage process.

Firstly, all the records are entered in the file regardless of their order (i.e. setting up a serial file).

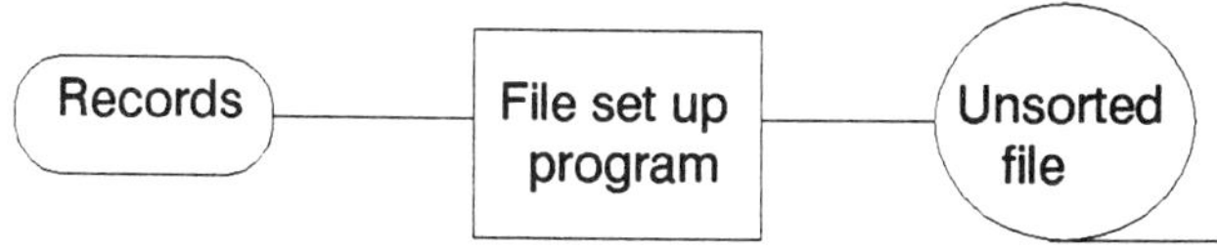

Secondly, having decided which is to be the **key** field and whether the records are to be held in ascending or descending order of that key, a sort program is run on the file producing a sorted file.

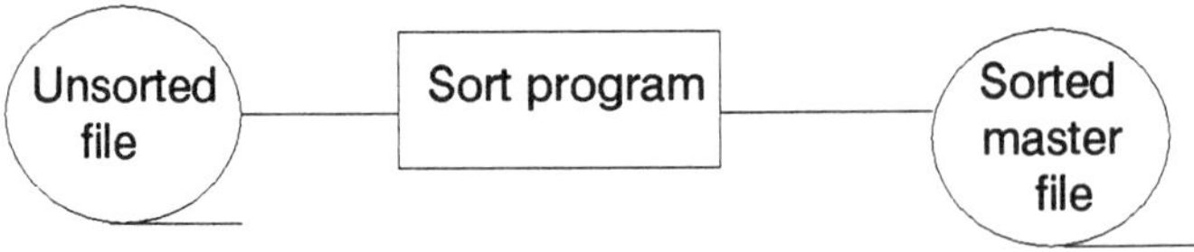

Adding Records To A Sequential File

When records are added to a sequential file they must be inserted in the correct place (determined by their key). As the records currently in the file are one after the other, the only way to make room for new records is to copy the file to another file inserting the new records in their appropriate place. Therefore, records are added to a sequential file by using a two stage process.

Firstly, new records are put onto a serial file and then sorted. This sorted file is called a **transaction** file.

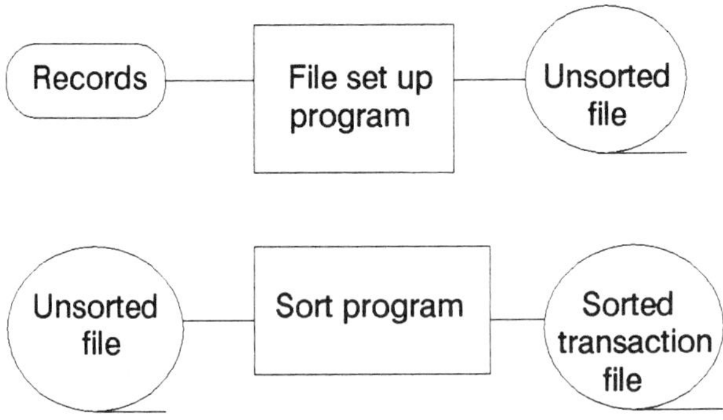

This should be recognised as being the same process that was used to set up the original **master** file. The only difference is that only those records that are being added to the file are being used.

Secondly, the file containing the sorted new records is merged with the **master** file to produce an **new** master file.

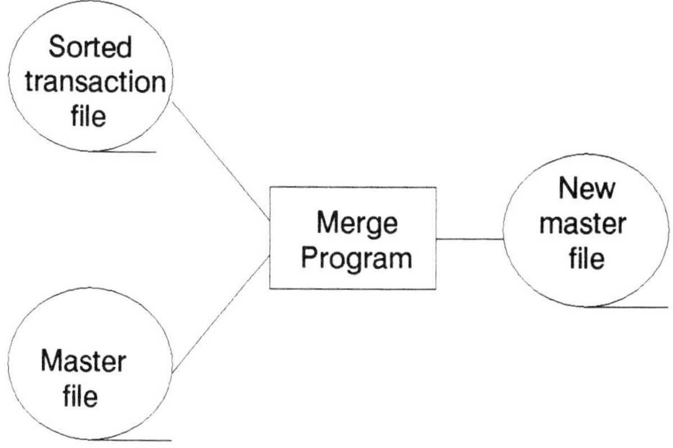

Deleting records from a sequential file

In order to delete records from a sequential file the appropriate records have to be found and removed from the file. As this would leave gaps in the file, where records were deleted, a similar process to that of adding records is used. That is, only those records to be retained in the file are copied to a new master file. Once again a two stage process is used.

Firstly, the record keys of those records that are to be deleted are determined and put into a file in sequential order. This file is then sorted to produce a file that contains the keys of the records to be deleted in the order that these records will occur in the file.

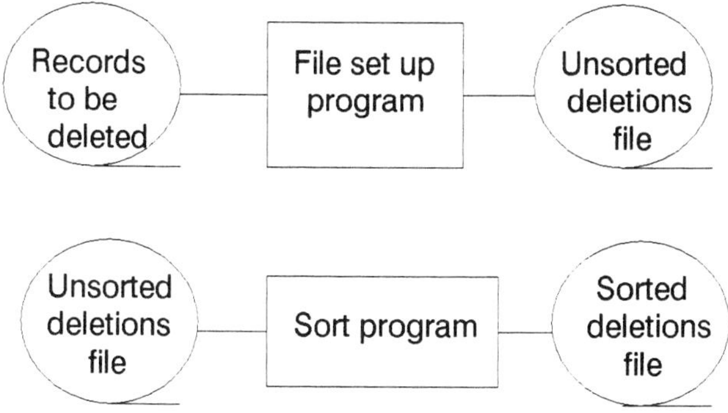

Secondly, the key of the record to be deleted is read from the sorted file. A record is then read from the master file, if it does **not** have the required record key then it is written to the new master. Those records with the required key are ignored.

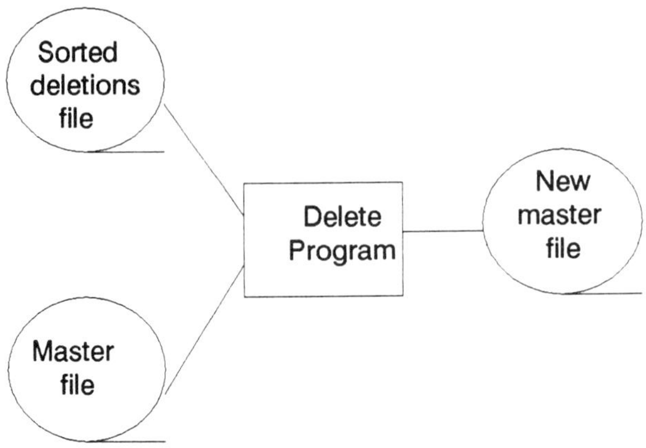

Processing a sequential file

A sequential file is processed by reading a record at a time. The record key is checked to see if it is the required record. If the record has a key that is greater than the required record then the required record is not in the file.

The next chapter shows how sequential file processing can be undertaken using the C programming language.

9 File Processing In C

Currently our TV Rental Program is restricted to a maximum of 50 customers. This could be increased to utilise all the remaining empty memory. However, as soon as the computer is switched off or another program is executed the customer information is lost and has to be re-entered. Both these problems can be overcome by storing the customer information on a disk file.

9.1 File Organisation

The basis of most file organisations is a **record**. In C a record can be formed using a **structure.** For example, in our TV Rental Program a record would contain all the information about one customer, which we have already defined as a **structure.**

Next, consideration has to be given to the order of the records within the file. For the present we will assume that they will be organised **sequentially** in order of customer number. That is the record for customer 3 will be before that of customer 10.

As we will not know in advance how many customer records are going to be put in the file we must have some method of knowing when we are at the end of a file. For our particular file we will write a record with a customer_no of 9999 at the end of the file. Hence when we read the record with the customer_no 9999 we will know that this is the last record on the file.

9.2 Setting Up Files

Returning to our TV rental Program, if we have all the information on our customers held in a file, then the program will take its input from a file rather than from the keyboard. This assumes that a file already exists containing the customer records. Therefore a program has to be written to set up this file. If we assume that the customer records are input, via the keyboard, in sequential order of customer number then the outline of this program will be

```
open file for output
while more customers
    input customer record
    write customer record to file
write end of file record to file
close file
```

If the customer records are put into a file called RENTAL then the TV Rental Set-up Program is

```
#include <stdio.h>

/* TV Rental File Set-up - Version 1
- Setting up a file containing customer information*/

struct customer_record        /*Defining a customer record*/
{
int customer_no;
int no_of_weeks;
char tv_type;
};

main()
{
struct customer_record customer;
char another_customer;

/*Declare fp_rental as a file pointer*/
FILE *fopen(), *fp_rental;

/*Open file for output*/
if ((fp_rental = fopen("rental", "w")) == = NULL)
{
printf("\nCannot open file 'rental' for writing\n");
printf("PROGRAM IS TERMINATED");
exit();
}

/*For each customer*/
do
{
/*Input customer details*/
customer_input(&customer);
```

```
        /*Write customer record to file rental*/
        fprintf(fp_rental, "%4d%2d%c\n", customer);

        /*Another customer record*/
        printf("\nAnother customer record for input (y or n)? ");
        scanf("%s", &another_customer);
    }
    while (another_customer = = 'y');

    /*Output end of file record*/
    fprintf(fp_rental, "%4d%2d%s\n", 9999, 99, ' ');

    /*Close file*/
    fclose(fp_rental);
}

customer_input(cust)        /*Input customer information*/
struct customer_record *cust;
{
    /*Input customer number and number of weeks rent due*/
    printf("\nEnter customer number ");
    scanf("%4d", & (*cust).customer_no);
    printf("Enter number of weeks rent due ");
    scanf("%2d", & (*cust).no_of_weeks);

    /*Input TV type*/
    printf("Enter type of rental - c for Colour TV");
    printf("\n                    b for Black and White TV ");
    printf("\n                    v for Video ");
    printf("\n                    o for other ");
    scanf("%s", & (*cust).tv_type);
}
```

Running this program gives:

Enter customer number **1111**
Enter number of weeks rent due **2**
Enter type of rental - c for Colour TV
b for Black and White TV
v for Video
o for other **c**

Another customer record for input (y or n)? **y**

```
Enter customer number **2222**
Enter number of weeks rent due **2**
Enter type of rental - c for Colour TV
                       b for Black and White TV
                       v for Video
                       o for other **b**

Another customer record for input (y or n)? **y**

Enter customer number **3333**
Enter number of weeks rent due **10**
Enter type of rental - c for Colour TV
                       b for Black and White TV
                       v for Vide
                       o for other **c**

Another customer record for input (y or n)? **y**

Enter customer number **4444**
Enter number of weeks rent due **2**
Enter type of rental - c for Colour TV
                       b for Black and White TV
                       v for Video
                       o for other **c**

Another customer record for input (y or n)? **y**

Enter customer number **5555**
Enter number of weeks rent due **1**
Enter type of rental - c for Colour TV
                       b for Black and White TV
                       v for Video
                       o for other **c**

Another customer record for input (y or n)? **n**
```

Try entering this program into your computer and running it. Remember to enter the records in order of customer number.

Check that the file has been written correctly by entering

```
type rental
```

in response to the operating system prompt (e.g. C>). This should give an output similar to

```
C>type rental
    1111 2c
    2222 2b
    333310c
    4444 2c
    5555 1c
    999999
```

Note that our structure does not include the variable bill, as this is calculated in our program and currently we are just concerned with input.

Now lets look at the file handling statements used in the file set up program.

Open A File

In order to use a file it must first be **opened**. For the TV Rental File Set-up Program we wish to open a **file** called **rental** into which a number of records are to be written. The C statement for this is

```
fp_rental = fopen("rental", "w")
```

A file **rental** is open in **write**(w) mode and a pointer to that file is returned and assigned to the pointer **fp_rental**.

The general form of the **fopen()** statement is

```
<file_pointer> = fopen(<file_name>, <access_mode>);
```

where the **<file_name> is a string of characters forming a valid filename and <access_mode> is one of**

w - open a file for information to be **written** to it. If the file already exists any information currently in it is overwritten.

a - open a file to allow records to be **added** to the end of it.

r - open a file to allow the records in it to be **read**.

As in some cases a file cannot be opened (e.g. lack of space on the disk, or the file does not already exist) it is therefore necessary to check that it has been opened before trying to use it.

Hence, as **fopen()** returns the value **NULL** if there are any problems opening the file, a check can easily be made by

```
if ((fp_rental = fopen("rental", "w")) = = NULL)
  {
  printf("\nCannot open file 'rental' for writing\n");
  printf("PROGRAM IS TERMINATED");
  exit();
  }
```

NB This is an allowable use of the function **exit()** as there is no point in continuing with the program if the file cannot be opened.

Closing A File

Before leaving a program files must be closed. It is also a good idea to close a file once it is finished with. Hence in our TV Rental File Set-up Program we have the statement

```
fclose(fp_rental);
```

This closes the file with the file pointer fp.

Writing To A File

Once a file has been opened for writing we can start to output records to it. This is done by using the **fprint()** function. For example,

```
fprintf(fp_rental, "%4d%2d%c\n", customer);
```

will output a 4 digit integer, followed by a 2 digit integer, followed by a single character all held in the variable customer (remember this is of type structure) to the file pointed at by the file pointer fp. The \n is used to mark the end of the record. (NB **fprint()** assumes a file has already been opened for either writing or appending.)

The general syntax of the **fprint()** function is

```
fprint(<file_pointer>, "<output_format>", <variable_list>);
```

9.3 Processing Information Held In A File

Returning to our TV Rental Program (the one that produces the customer bills). Firstly, the function customer_input() has to be re-written to take the customer records from the file **rental** rather than from the keyboard. For example,

```
fscanf(fp_rent, "%4d%2d%c\n", &customer.customer_no,
              &customer.no_of_weeks, &customer.tv_type);
```

will read a record with the format %4d%2d%c from the file pointed at by the file pointer fp and puts it in the variables listed. (NB see section 1.4 as fscanf() uses the same formats as scanf().)

The general syntax is

```
fscanf(<file_pointer>, "<input_format>", <variable_list>);
```

The pseudo code for the TV Rental Program will now be

```
open files - old master(read), temporay file(write)
while not end-of-file
    read customers record from master file
    process bill
    output customers bill
    write customers bill information to temporary file
close files
open temporary file(read)
output summary report
close temporary file
```

Where the **master** file is the existing file **rental** and the **temporary** file, **summ** will contain a copy of the existing record together with the rent due for each customer. The summary report will then be produced using the information in this file.

The bill is converted to a whole number before being output to the file and converted back to a monetary value (i.e. two decimal places) when read back from the file.

Remember that the file will have to be closed once all the summary information has been written to it and then reopened in read mode to allow this information to be read for the report. This effectively repositions the file pointer to the start of the file.

Once the TV Rental Program has been executed this temporary file can be over written.

Changing the TV Rental Program to read the customer information from a file gives

```
#include <stdio.h>

/* TV Rental Billing - Version 17
 - Processing customer information from a file*/

struct customer_record        /*Defining a customer record*/
     {
     int customer_no;
     int no_of_weeks;
     char tv_type;
     };

main()
{
    struct customer_record customer;
    int rent_out;
    float rent_per_week, rent_due, weeks_rental();

    /*Declare fp_rent and fp_summ as file pointers*/
    FILE *fopen(), *fp_rent, *fp_summ;

    /*Open files - rental for reading and summ for writing*/
    if ((fp_rent = fopen("rental", "r")) == NULL)
      {
      printf("\n\nCannot open file 'rental' for reading\n");
      printf("PROGRAM IS TERMINATED");
      exit();
      }

    if ((fp_summ = fopen("summ", "w")) == NULL)
      {
      printf("\n\nCannot open file 'summ' for writing\n");
      printf("PROGRAM IS TERMINATED");
      exit();
      }

    /*Process customers bills*/
    do
      {
      /*Input customer record*/
      fscanf(fp_rent, "%4d%2d%c\n", &customer.customer_no,
                  &customer.no_of_weeks, &customer.tv_type);

      /*if end of file customer number is 9999*/
```

```
        if (customer.customer_no != 9999)
          {
          /*Determine rent due*/
          rent_per_week = weeks_rental(&customer, &rent_due);

          /*Converting rent_due to integer ready for output to the
            file. At this stage rounding errors may occur, hence the
            addition of 0.005*/
          rent_out = (rent_due + 0.005) * 100;

          /*Output information to summary file - summ*/
          fprintf(fp_summ, "%4d%2d%c%6d\n", customer, rent_out);

          /*Print the bill*/
          if (rent_per_week != 0)
            print_bill(&customer, rent_per_week, rent_due);
          }
        }
    while(customer.customer_no != 9999);

    /*Output end of file record to file summ*/
    fprintf(fp_summ, "%4d%2d%c%6d\n", 9999, 99, ' ', 9999);

    /*Close files*/
    fclose(fp_rent);
    fclose(fp_summ);

    /*Calculate and output summary table*/
    summary();
}

float weeks_rental(cust,due)          /*Determine rent per week*/
struct customer_record *cust;
float *due;
{
    /*Rent per week*/
    switch ((*cust).tv_type)
    {
    case 'c': /*Colour TV rental is 3.60*/
          *due = (*cust).no_of_weeks*3.60;
          return(3.60);
    case 'b': /*Black and white TV rental is 1.75*/
          *due = (*cust).no_of_weeks*1.75;
          return(1.75);
```

```
    case 'v': /*Video rental is 1.50*/
          *due = (*cust).no_of_weeks*1.50;
          return(1.50);
    default : /*Illegal input for tv_type*/
          printf("\n\nProgram does not handle this type of rental\n\n");
          return(0);
    }
}

print_bill(cust, rent,due)          /*Calculate and print the bill*/
struct customer_record *cust;
float rent, due;
{
    printf("\n\nTV RENTAL BILL");
    printf("\n\nCustomer number is %d", (*cust).customer_no);
    printf("\nNumber of weeks rent due is %d", (*cust).no_of_weeks);
    printf("\nRent per week is %.2f", rent);
    printf("\n\nRental due is %.2f\n\n", due);
}

summary()     /*Produce summary report*/
{
    struct customer_record cust;
    float total, rent_due;
    int rent;

    FILE *fp_summ;  /*Declares fp_summ as a file pointer*/

    total = 0;    /*Initialise total*/

    /*Open file - summ for reading*/
    if ((fp_summ = fopen("summ", "r")) == = NULL)
      {
      printf("\n\nCannot open file 'summ' for reading\n");
      printf("PROGRAM IS TERMINATED");
      exit();
      }

    /*Print table headings*/
    printf("\n\n              SUMMARY REPORT");
    printf("\n              --------------");
    printf("\n\nCustomer number  Weeks due  Rental type  Rent due");
    printf("\n---------------  ---------  -----------  --------");
```

```
    /*Output summary table*/
    do
      {
      /*Read customer information from file summ*/
      fscanf(fp_summ ,"%4d%2d%c%6d\n", &cust.customer_no,
                       &cust.no_of_weeks, &cust.tv_type, &rent);

      /*If end of file customer number is 9999*/
      if (cust.customer_no != 9999)
        {
        /*Rent due was written to the file as an integer
          therefore has to be converted back to a floating
          point number*/
        rent_due = rent / 100.0;

        /*Print table of customer information*/
        printf("\n     %4d        %2d        %c      %6.2f",
                                         cust, rent_due);

        /*Calculate total rent due*/
        total = total + rent_due;
        }
      }
    while (cust.customer_no != 9999);

    /*Close file*/
    fclose(fp_summ);

    /*Print total rent due*/
    printf("\n\n               Total rent due is %12.2f\n\n", total);
}
```

Running this program gives:

TV RENTAL BILL

Customer number is 1111
Number of weeks rent due is 2
Rent per week is 3.60

Rental due is 7.20

TV RENTAL BILL

Customer number is 2222
Number of weeks rent due is 2
Rent per week is 1.75

Rental due is 3.50

TV RENTAL BILL

Customer number is 3333
Number of weeks rent due is 10
Rent per week is 3.60

Rental due is 36.00

TV RENTAL BILL

Customer number is 4444
Number of weeks rent due is 2
Rent per week is 3.60

Rental due is 7.20

TV RENTAL BILL

Customer number is 5555
Number of weeks rent due is 1
Rent per week is 3.60

Rental due is 3.60

SUMMARY REPORT

Customer number	Weeks due	Rental type	Rent due
1111	2	c	7.20
2222	2	b	3.50
3333	10	c	36.00

4444	2	c	7.20
5555	1	c	3.60
Total rent due is			57.50

Adding Records To A File

Records are added to a sequential file by inserting them in their correct place based on their sequential key. For example, if a file is ordered on customer_no and already contains records for customer_no 10 and 15. A new customer_no 12 will be inserted between the existing records.

As space has not been left in the original file to allow new records to be inserted a new file is created into which the new records are written in their correct place as the old file is copied across. If we assume that the records to be inserted are in customer number order then the process for adding records to a file is

```
open files - old master, new master
read new customer_info
read record from old master file

while not at end of old master file

    while customer_info_no > record_no

        output record to new master file
        read record from old master file
        if EOF
            output customer_info to new master file
            while more new customers
                read new customer_info
                output customer_info to new master file
            output EOF record to new master file

    while customer_info_no < record_no

        output customer_info to new master file
        if more new customers
            read customer_info
        else
            output record to new master file
            while not EOF
```

read record from old master file
output record to new master file

close files

Once the new master file has been created it must be given the same filename as the old master file or the programs will not work. This is done within the program by deleting the old master file using the C function

```
unlink(<filename>);
```

The new master file can then be renamed using the C function

```
rename(<old_file_name>, <new_file_name>);
```

Hence a program for adding records to the file rental for the TV Rental Program is

```
#include <stdio.h>

* TV Rental File Additions - Version 1*/

struct customer_record      /*Defining a customer record*/
    {
    int customer_no;
    int no_of_weeks;
    char tv_type;
    };

main()
   {
   struct customer_record customer;

   /*Declare file pointers*/
   FILE *fopen(), *fp_rental, *fp_rentout;

   /*Open file for input*/
   if ((fp_rental = fopen("rental", "r")) = = NULL)
     {
     printf("\n\nCannot open file 'rental' for writing\n");
     printf("PROGRAM IS TERMINATED");
     exit();
     }
```

```
    /*Open file for output*/
    if ((fp_rentout = fopen("rentout", "w")) = = NULL)
    {
        printf("\n\nCannot open file 'rentout' for writing\n");
        printf("PROGRAM IS TERMINATED");
        exit();
    }

    /*Update new master file*/
    update(fp_rental, fp_rentout);

    /*Close files*/
    fclose(fp_rental);
    fclose(fp_rentout);

    /*Delete old master file*/
    unlink("rental");

    /*Rename new master to old masters name*/
    rename("rentout", "rental");
}

update(fp_in, fp_out)      /*Add customer record to file*/
FILE *fp_in, *fp_out;
{
    struct customer_record customer, record;

    /*Input customer record*/
    customer_input(&customer);

    /*Input record from the old master file*/
    fscanf(fp_in, "%4d%2d%c\n", &record.customer_no,
    &record.no_of_weeks, &record.tv_type);

    do
    {
        while (customer.customer_no > record.customer_no)
        {
            /*Output record to new master file*/
            fprintf(fp_out, "%4d%2d%c\n", record);

            /*Input record from the old master file*/
            fscanf(fp_in, "%4d%2d%c\n", &record.customer_no,
            &record.no_of_weeks, &record.tv_type);
```

```
    if (record.customer_no = = 9999)
    {
        /*Output customer record to new master file*/
        fprintf(fp_out, "%4d%2d%c\n", customer);

        /*Output any remaining customer records*/
        while (another_customer() = = 'y')
        {
            /*Input customer record*/
            customer_input(&customer);

            /*Output new customer to new master file*/
            fprintf(fp_out, "%4d%2d%c\n", customer);
        }
        /*No more new customers*/
        customer.customer_no = 9999;

        /*Write end of file record to new master file*/
        fprintf(fp_out, "%4d%2d%c\n", record);
    }
}
while (customer.customer_no < record.customer_no)
{
    /*Output new customer to new master file*/
    fprintf(fp_out, "%4d%2d%c\n", customer);

    /*If more new customers*/
    if (another_customer() = = 'y')
        /*Input customer record*/
        customer_input(&customer);
    else
    {
        /*No more new customers*/
        customer.customer_no = 9999;

        /*Output record to new master file*/
        fprintf(fp_out, "%4d%2d%c\n", record);

        /*Output records remaining to new master file*/
        while (record.customer_no != 9999)
        {
            /*Input record from the old master file*/
            fscanf(fp_in, "%4d%2d%c\n", &record.customer_no,
                        &record.no_of_weeks, &record.tv_type);
```

```
                /*Output record to new master file*/
                fprintf(fp_out, "%4d%2d%c\n", record);
            }
        }
    }
   }
   while (record.customer_no ! = 9999);
}

customer_input(cust)          /*Input customer information*/
struct customer_record *cust;
{
    /*Input customer number and number of weeks rent due*/
    printf("\nEnter customer number ");
    scanf("%4d", & (*cust).customer_no);
    printf("Enter number of weeks rent due ");
    scanf("%2d", & (*cust).no_of_weeks);

    /*Input TV type*/
    printf("Enter type of rental - c for Colour TV");
    printf("\n                    b for Black and White TV ");
    printf("\n                    v for Video ");
    printf("\n                    o for other ");
    scanf("%s", &(*cust).tv_type);
}

another_customer()    /*Is there another customer to be added to file*/
{
    char another;

    printf("\nAnother customer record to be added (y or n)? ");
    scanf("%s", &another);
    return(another);
}
```

Running this program gives:

Enter customer number **700**
Enter number of weeks rent due **3**
Enter type of rental - c for Colour TV
b for Black and white TV
v for Video
o for other **c**

Another customer record to be added (y or n)? **y**

Enter customer number **1000**
Enter number of weeks rent due **2**
Enter type of rental - c for Colour TV
b for Black and white TV
v for Video
o for other **c**

Another customer record to be added (y or n)? **y**

Enter customer number **1500**
Enter number of weeks rent due **2**
Enter type of rental - c for Colour TV
b for Black and white TV
v for Video
o for other **c**

Another customer record to be added (y or n)? **y**

Enter customer number **4000**
Enter number of weeks rent due **3**
Enter type of rental - c for Colour TV
b for Black and white TV
v for Video
o for other **b**

Another customer record to be added (y or n)? **y**

Enter customer number **7000**
Enter number of weeks rent due **4**
Enter type of rental - c for Colour TV
b for Black and white TV
v for Video
o for other **c**

Another customer record to be added (y or n)? **y**

Enter customer number **8000**
Enter number of weeks rent due **2**
Enter type of rental - c for Colour TV
b for Black and white TV
v for Video
o for other **v**

Another customer record to be added (y or n)? **y**

Enter customer number **8100**
Enter number of weeks rent due **3**
Enter type of rental - c for Colour TV
b for Black and white TV
v for Video
o for other **b**

Another customer record to be added (y or n)? **n**

Listing the file rental gives:

700 3c
1000 2c
1111 2c
1500 4c
2222 2b
333310c
4000 3b
4444 2c
5555 1c
7000 4c
8000 2v
8100 3b
999999

Testing File Processing Programs

When testing programs that process files there are four general cases that must be considered. Records

- at the beginning of the file
- at the end of the file
- elsewhere in the file
- not in the file

Also, in each case consideration should be given to both a single record and multiple records occurring within each of the above.

Deleting Records From A File

If customers cancel their rental then their record will need to be removed (i.e. deleted) from the customer file.

This is done by copying all the records that are not to be deleted to a new file and then renaming that file. Assuming that the customer_no of the records to be deleted are entered via the keyboard in customer_no order then this process is

```
open files  -  old master, new master
read customer_no to be deleted
read record from old master file

while not at the end of old master file

    while customer_no = record_no
        if more customer deletions
            read customer_no
            read record from old master file
        else
            while not EOF
                read record from old master file
                output record to new master file

    while customer_no > record_no
        output record to new master file
        read record from old master file
        if EOF
            ERROR - Customer record not on file
            output EOF to new master file

    while customer_no < record_no
        ERROR - Customer record not on file
        if more customer deletions
            read customer_no

close files
```

Based on this pseudo code the deletions program for the TV Rental System is

```
#include <stdio.h>

/* TV Rental File Deletions - Version 1*/

struct customer_record        /*Defining a customer record*/
     {
     int customer_no;
     int no_of_weeks;
     char tv_type;
     };

main()
    {
    struct customer_record customer;

    /*Declare file pointers*/
    FILE *fopen(), *fp_rental, *fp_rentout;

    /*Open file for input*/
    if ((fp_rental = fopen("rental", "r")) = = NULL)
      {
      printf("\n\nCannot open file 'rental' for writing\n");
      printf("PROGRAM IS TERMINATED");
      exit();
      }

    /*Open file for output*/
    if ((fp_rentout = fopen("rentout", "w")) = = NULL)
      {
      printf("\n\nCannot open file 'rentout' for writing\n");
      printf("PROGRAM IS TERMINATED");
      exit();
      }

    /*Delete records from master file*/
    delete(fp_rental, fp_rentout);

    /*Close files*/
    fclose(fp_rental);
    fclose(fp_rentout);

    /*Delete old master file*/
    unlink("rental");
```

```
    /*Rename new master to old masters name*/
    rename("rentout", "rental");
}

delete(fp_in, fp_out)      /*Delete customer records from file*/
FILE *fp_in, *fp_out;
{
    struct customer_record record;
    int customer_no;

    /*Input customer number of record to be deleted*/
    customer_input(&customer_no);

    /*Input record from the old master file*/
    fscanf(fp_in, "%4d%2d%c\n", &record.customer_no,
                   &record.no_of_weeks, &record.tv_type);

    do
     {
      while ((customer_no = = record.customer_no) &&
                        (record.customer_no != 9999))
      {
         /*If more customers to be deleted*/
         if (another_customer() = = 'y')
           {
           /*Input number of customer to be deleted*/
           customer_input(&customer_no);

           /*Input record from the old master file*/
           fscanf(fp_in, "%4d%2d%c\n", &record.customer_no,
                   &record.no_of_weeks, &record.tv_type);
           }
         else
           {
           /*No more customer deletions*/
           customer_no = 9999;

           /*Output records remaining to new master file*/
           while (record.customer_no != 9999)
           {
             /*Input record from the old master file*/
             fscanf(fp_in, "%4d%2d%c\n", &record.customer_no,
                     &record.no_of_weeks, &record.tv_type);
```

```
        /*Output record to new master file*/
        fprintf(fp_out, "%4d%2d%c\n", record);
      }
      }
}

while (customer_no > record.customer_no)
{
   /*Output record to new master file*/
   fprintf(fp_out, "%4d%2d%c\n", record);

   /*Input record from the old master file*/
   fscanf(fp_in, "%4d%2d%c\n", &record.customer_no,
            &record.no_of_weeks, &record.tv_type);

   if (record.customer_no = = 9999)
     {
     /*Error EOF, deletion not found*/
     printf("\nERROR - Customer record %4d not found",
                        customer_no);
     printf("\nEnd of file reached - Program terminated\n");

     /*No more customer deletions*/
     customer_no = 9999;

     /*Write end of file record to new master file*/
     fprintf(fp_out, "%4d%2d%c\n", record);
     }
}

while (customer_no < record.customer_no)
{
   /*Deletion not found*/
   printf("\nERROR - Customer record %4d not found\n",
                        customer_no);

   if (record.customer_no = = 9999)
     {
     /*End of file*/
     printf("End of file reached - Program terminated\n");

     /*No more customer deletions*/
     customer_no = 9999;
```

```
            /*Write end of file record to new master file*/
            fprintf(fp_out, "%4d%2d%c\n", record);
            }
          /*If more customers to be deleted*/
          else if (another_customer() = = 'y')
              /*Input number of customer to be deleted*/
              customer_input(&customer_no);
            else
              /*No more deletions*/
              customer_no = 9999;
      }
    }
    while (record.customer_no ! = 9999);
}

customer_input(cust_no)         /*Input number of customer to be deleted*/
int *cust_no;
{
   printf("Enter customer number of record to be deleted ");
   scanf("%4d", cust_no);
}

another_customer()    /*Another customer record to be deleted*/
{
   char another;

   printf("\nAnother customer record to be deleted (y or n)? ");
   scanf("%s", &another);
   return(another);
}
```

Running this program gives:

Enter customer number of record to be deleted **700**

Another customer record to be deleted (y or n)? **y**
Enter customer number of record to be deleted **1700**

ERROR - Customer record 1700 not found

Another customer record to be deleted (y or n)? **y**
Enter customer number of record to be deleted **4444**

Another customer record to be deleted (y or n)? **y**

Enter customer number of record to be deleted **5555**

Another customer record to be deleted (y or n)? **y**
Enter customer number of record to be deleted **7000**

Another customer record to be deleted (y or n)? **y**
Enter customer number of record to be deleted **8100**

Another customer record to be deleted (y or n)? **y**
Enter customer number of record to be deleted **9000**

ERROR - Customer record 9000 not found

End of file reached - Program terminated

Listing the file rental gives:

1000 2c
1111 2c
2222 2b
333310c
4000 3b
8000 2v
999999

Amending File Records

It should be obvious that in the TV Rental application the number of weeks for which the rent is due will vary from one payment to the next. Hence, it is necessary to be able to **amend** individual records in the file rental. Only those records where the number of weeks rent due has changed will need to be amended. This means that individual records will need to be identified. Therefore, in order to carry out the appropriate amendment we will need to know

- the customer number (identifies the record)
- number of weeks rent now due

If we assume that this information is entered via the keyboard in customer number order then the process for carrying out the amendments will be

```
open files - old master, new master
read customer_no to be deleted
read record from old master file
while not at end of old master file

    while customer_no = record_no
        input changes to record
        output new customer_onfo to new master
        if more customer deletions
            read customer_no
            read record from old master
        else
            while not EOF
                read record from old master file
                output record to new master file

    while customer_no > record_no
        output record to new master file
        read record from old master file
        if EOF
            ERROR - Customer record not on file
            output EOF to new master

    while customer_no < record_no
        ERROR - Customer record not on file
        if more customer deletions
            read customer_no

close files
```

Based on this pseudo code a program for adding amendments to the TV Rental System file is

```
#include <stdio.h>

/* TV Rental File Ammendments - Version 1*/

struct customer_record        /*Defining a customer record*/
    {
    int customer_no;
    int no_of_weeks;
    char tv_type;
    };
```

```
main()
{
    struct customer_record customer;

    /*Declare file pointers*/
    FILE *fopen(), *fp_rental, *fp_rentout;

    /*Open file for input*/
    if ((fp_rental = fopen("rental", "r")) = = NULL)
      {
      printf("\n\nCannot open file 'rental' for writing\n");
      printf("PROGRAM IS TERMINATED");
      exit();
      }

    /*Open file for output*/
    if ((fp_rentout = fopen("rentout", "w")) = = NULL)
      {
      printf("\n\nCannot open file 'rentout' for writing\n");
      printf("PROGRAM IS TERMINATED");
      exit();
      }

    /*Change records in master file*/
    change(fp_rental, fp_rentout);

    /*Close files*/
    fclose(fp_rental);
    fclose(fp_rentout);

    /*Delete old master file*/
    unlink("rental");

    /*Rename new master to old masters name*/
    rename("rentout", "rental");
}

change(fp_in, fp_out)      /*Change customer records in file*/
FILE *fp_in, *fp_out;
    {
    struct customer_record customer, record;

    /*Input customer number of record to be changed*/
    customer_input(&customer.customer_no);
```

```
/*Input record from the old master file*/
fscanf(fp_in, "%4d%2d%c\n", &record.customer_no,
                &record.no_of_weeks, &record.tv_type);

do
 {
  while ((customer.customer_no = = record.customer_no) &&
                   (record.customer_no ! = 9999))
  {
     /*Input changes to customer record*/
     alter_customer_input(&customer);

     /*Output changed record to file*/
     fprintf(fp_out, "%4d%2d%c\n", customer);

     /*If more customer records to be changed*/
     if (another_customer() = = 'y')
       {
       /*Input number of customer to be altered*/
       customer_input(&customer.customer_no);

       /*Input record from the old master file*/
       fscanf(fp_in, "%4d%2d%c\n", &record.customer_no,
               &record.no_of_weeks, &record.tv_type);
       }
     else
       {
       /*No more customer alterations*/
       customer.customer_no = 9999;

       /*Output records remaining to new master file*/
       while (record.customer_no ! = 9999)
       {
          /*Input record from the old master file*/
          fscanf(fp_in, "%4d%2d%c\n", &record.customer_no,
                  &record.no_of_weeks, &record.tv_type);

          /*Output record to new master file*/
          fprintf(fp_out, "%4d%2d%c\n", record);
       }
       }
  }

  while (customer.customer_no > record.customer_no)
```

```
{
    /*Output record to new master file*/
    fprintf(fp_out, "%4d%2d%c\n", record);

    /*Input record from the old master file*/
    fscanf(fp_in, "%4d%2d%c\n", &record.customer_no,
                &record.no_of_weeks, &record.tv_type);

    if (record.customer_no = = 9999)
      {
      /*Error EOF, record to be changed not found*/
      printf("\nERROR - Customer record %4d not found",
                          customer.customer_no);
      printf("\nEnd of file reached - Program terminated\n");

      /*No more customer alterations*/
      customer.customer_no = 9999;

      /*Write end of file record to new master file*/
      fprintf(fp_out, "%4d%2d%c\n", record);
      }
}

while (customer.customer_no < record.customer_no)
{
    /*Record to be changed not found*/
    printf("\nERROR - Customer record %4d not found",
                        customer.customer_no);

    if (record.customer_no = = 9999)
      {
      /*End of file found*/
      printf("\nEnd of file reached - Program terminated\n");

      /*No more customer alterations*/
      customer.customer_no = 9999;

      /*Write end of file record to new master file*/
      fprintf(fp_out, "%4d%2d%c\n", record);
      }
    /*If more customer records to be altered*/
    else if (another_customer() = = 'y')
      /*Input number of customer record to be changed*/
      customer_input(&customer.customer_no);
```

```
            else
              /*No more alterations*/
              customer.customer_no = 9999;
        }
      }
      while (record.customer_no ! = 9999);
}

customer_input(cust_no)     /*Input number of customer to be altered*/
int *cust_no;
{
    printf("Enter number of customer record to be altered ");
    scanf("%4d", cust_no);
}

another_customer()    /*Another customer record to be altered*/
{
    char another;
    printf("\nAnother customer record to be altered (y or n)? ");
    scanf("%s", &another);
    return(another);
}

alter_customer_input(cust)     /*Input changes to customer information*/
struct customer_record *cust;
{
    /*Input required changes*/
    printf("\nEnter changes, as follows");

    /*Input number of weeks rent due*/
    printf("\nEnter number of weeks rent due ");
    scanf("%2d", & (*cust).no_of_weeks);

    /*Input TV type*/
    printf("Enter type of rental - c for Colour TV");
    printf("\n                    b for Black and White TV ");
    printf("\n                    v for Video ");
    printf("\n                    o for other ");
    scanf("%s", &(*cust).tv_type);
}
```

Running this program gives:

Enter number of customer record to be altered **1000**

Enter changes as follows
Enter number of weeks rent due **3**
Enter type of rental - c for Colour TV
b for Black and white TV
v for Video
o for other **c**

Another customer record to be altered (y or n)? **y**
Enter number of customer record to be altered **1111**

Enter changes as follows
Enter number of weeks rent due **3**
Enter type of rental - c for Colour TV
b for Black and white TV
v for Video
o for other **c**

Another customer record to be altered (y or n)? **y**
Enter number of customer record to be altered **3333**

Enter changes as follows
Enter number of weeks rent due **1**
Enter type of rental - c for Colour TV
b for Black and white TV
v for Video
o for other **c**

Another customer record to be altered (y or n)? **y**
Enter number of customer record to be altered **3500**

ERROR - Customer record 3500 not found
Another customer record to be altered (y or n)? **y**
Enter number of customer record to be altered **8200**

Enter changes as follows
Enter number of weeks rent due **3**
Enter type of rental - c for Colour TV
b for Black and white TV
v for Video
o for other **v**

Another customer record to be altered (y or n)? **y**
Enter number of customer record to be altered **9000**

```
ERROR - Customer record 9000 not found
End of file reached - Program terminated
```

Listing file rental gives:

```
1000 3c
1111 3c
2222 2b
3333 1c
4000 3b
8000 3v
999999
```

Displaying A Single Record

Often in a file based system there is a requirement to display a single record. For example in the TV Rental System we may wish to know what a particular customer rents. This information could be obtained by finding and displaying the relevant record. Hence this operation is carried out by

```
open file - master
input customer_no of required record
while not EOF
    read customer_record
    if EOF
        ERROR - Customer record not on file
    else if customer_no = customer_record
            display customer record
close file
```

Based on this pseudo code a program for the TV Rental Program system that will display any customer record on request is

```
#include <stdio.h>

/* TV Rental Display Customer Record - Version 1*/

struct customer_record        /*Defining a customer record*/
    {
    int customer_no;
    int no_of_weeks;
    char tv_type;
```

```
    };

main()
{
    struct customer_record customer;
    int display_customer_no;

    /*Declare fp as a file pointer*/
    FILE *fopen(), *fp;

    /*Open file for reading*/
    if ((fp = fopen("rental", "r")) = = NULL)
      {
      printf("\n\nCannot open file 'rental' for writing\n");
      printf("PROGRAM IS TERMINATED");
      exit();
      }

    /*Input customer_no of record to be displayed*/
    input_customer_no(&display_customer_no);

    /*Find record to be displayed*/
    do
      {
      /*Read record from the file*/
      fscanf(fp, "%4d%2d%c\n", &customer.customer_no,
               &customer.no_of_weeks, &customer.tv_type);
      }
    while((customer.customer_no != display_customer_no) &&
                      (customer.customer_no != 9999));

    /*Close file*/
    fclose(fp);

    /*If end of file output an error message,
     other wise display record*/
    if (customer.customer_no = = 9999)
      no_record(display_customer_no);
    else
      display_record(&customer);
}

input_customer_no(cust)    /*Input customer no of record to be displayed*/
int *cust;
```

```
{
    printf("Enter customer number of record to be displayed ");
    scanf("%4d", cust);
}

no_record(cust)          /*No record for customer*/
int cust;
{
    printf("\nThere is no record for customer %4d on file\n", cust);
}

display_record(cust)     /*Display required customers record*/
struct customer_record *cust;
{
    printf("\nCustomer number %4d", (*cust).customer_no);
    printf("\nNumber of weeks rent due %2d", (*cust).no_of_weeks);
    printf("\nTV type %c\n", (*cust).tv_type);
}
```

Running this program gives:

Enter customer number of record to be displayed **3333**

Customer number 3333
Number of weeks rent due is 1
TV type c

Running this program gives:

Enter customer number of record to be displayed **1000**

Customer number 1000
Number of weeks rent due is 3
TV type c

Running this program gives:

Enter customer number of record to be displayed **8000**

Customer number 8000
Number of weeks rent due is 3
TV type v

Running this program gives:

Enter customer number of record to be displayed **7000**

There is no record for customer 7000 on file

9.4 Limitations Of The TV Rental Program

It must be remembered that within the TV Rental System there are no checks carried out on input, either (i) to ensure that the input is valid, or (ii) to check that all the inputs from the keyboard are in sequential order of customer_no.

In a real system checks must be included to ensure both the validity of the input and the sequence of entry. The easiest way of doing this is to

- read all input records to a file in any order, carrying out validity checks.
- to sort this file into the appropriate sequential order.

These two steps are equally valid for file set-ups, additions, deletions and amendments to any sequential filing system.

9.5 Programming Exercises

Solutions to the following exercises are not included in this book.

1. Alter the TV Rental Programs so that the customer information includes:
   - customer name
   - customer address

(Note that if these are input as strings any space within them will act as a terminator. Therefore set up the string in character array by inputting one character at a time using getc()).

2. Write a suite of programs to administer a mailing list containing contact name, address and telephone number.

9.6 Passing File Names To Programs

The way our TV Rental Programs are currently written means that they will only operate on a file called rental. If we want to change the name of the file then we have to change the file name in the **fopen()** statements. It would file then we have to change the file name in the **fopen()** statements. It would be much better if the filename was a variable which could be given a value every time the programs were run.

C allows us to pass information to a program when the program is initiated. For example, if the customer information is in a file called customer and the program for producing the TV Rental Bills is in a file called tv.exe then C allows us t pass the file name by entering

```
tv customer
```

to the operating system prompt (e.g. C>).

However, we have still to incorporate this into our program. Up until now the function main() has had no arguments, however it is possible to include two built-in arguments **argv** and **argc** (referred to as **command line arguments**).

argc contains the number of arguments in the command line (including the program name).

For example, for

```
tv customer
```

argc will have the value 2.

argv is a pointer to an array of strings, each element of which contains one argument. The number of elements in the array is equal to argc.

For example,

```
argc[0]=tv
argc[1]=customer
```

However, argc and argv must be incorporated into main() such that

```
main(argc, argv)
int argc
char *argv;
```

and the **fopen()** function call is now

```
fp = fopen(argv[1],"w");
```

Re-writing the TV Rental System File Set-up program written to use command line arguments gives

```
#include <stdio.h>

/* TV Rental File Set-up - Version 2
  - Setting up a file containing customer information
   - Using command line arguments for file name*/

struct customer_record        /*Defining a customer record*/
     {
     int customer_no;
     int no_of_weeks;
     char tv_type;
     };

main(argc,argv)
/*Passing the file name as part of the command line*/
int argc;
char *argv[];
{
    struct customer_record customer;
    char another_customer;

    /*Declare fp_rental as a file pointer*/
    FILE  *fopen(), *fp_rental;

    /*Open file for output*/
    if ((fp_rental = fopen(argv[1], "w")) == NULL)
      {
      printf("\nCannot open file %s for writing\n", argv[1]);
      printf("PROGRAM IS TERMINATED");
      exit();
      }

    /*For each customer*/
    do
      {
      /*Input customer details*/
      customer_input(&customer);

      /*Write customer record to file rental*/
      fprintf(fp_rental, "%4d%2d%c\n", customer);

      /*Another customer record*/
      printf("\nAnother customer record for input (y or n)? ");
      scanf("%s", &another_customer);
```

```
    }
    while (another_customer = = 'y');

    /*Output end of file record*/
    fprintf(fp_rental, "%4d%2d%s\n", 9999, 99, ' ');

    /*Close file*/
    fclose(fp_rental);
}

customer_input(cust)        /*Input customer information*/
struct customer_record *cust;
{
    /*Input customer number and number of weeks rent due*/
    printf("\nEnter customer number ");
    scanf("%4d", & (*cust).customer_no);
    printf("Enter number of weeks rent due ");
    scanf("%2d", & (*cust).no_of_weeks);

    /*Input TV type*/
    printf("Enter type of rental - c for Colour TV");
    printf("\n                     b for Black and White TV ");
    printf("\n                     v for Video ");
    printf("\n                     o for other ");
    scanf("%s", & (*cust).tv_type);
}
```

If this program is held in the file TVSETUP and the customer information is to go into a file called RENTAL then

```
        TVSETUP RENTAL
```

will result in

```
Enter customer number 100
Enter number of weeks rent due 4
Enter type of rental - c for Colour TV
                       b for Black and White TV
                       v for Video
                       o for other v

Another customer record for input (y or n)? y

Enter customer number 200
```

Enter number of weeks rent due **5**
Enter type of rental - c for Colour TV
b for Black and White TV
v for Video
o for other **c**

Another customer record for input (y or n)? **y**

Enter customer number **400**
Enter number of weeks rent due **1**
Enter type of rental - c for Colour TV
b for Black and White TV
v for Video
o for other **c**

Another customer record for input (y or n)? **n**

Listing the file RENTAL gives:

100 4v
200 5c
400 1c
999999

Now change the rest of the TV Rental programs to use command line arguments. There is no need for the output file to be included as this is just a temporary file used during the program and renamed to the original file at the end of the program. For example, if the old master file is 'rental' and the new master is 'rentout' then the old master file is deleted and the new master is renamed 'rental'. Hence 'rental' is the only file name that the user need be concerned with.

However, to do this both the C functions **unlink()** and **rename()** have to be altered to use command line arguments. Hence

```
unlink(argv[1]);

rename("rentout", argv[1]);
```

9.7 Programming Exercises

1. Alter the programs from section 9.5 to use command line arguments for the filenames.

10 Menu Driven Programs

It should be obvious from the previous chapter that once an application starts to use files a number of different programs are required. For example, file set up, file additions, file deletions, file amendments, file processing and displaying individual records.

As each of these programs are held in a file it means that the user of the application will have to become familiar with a number of different file names (which being restricted in the number of characters allowed may not be very meaningful). It would be much better if there was a single program that would assist the user in running the application. Hence the user would only have to specify one program name.

The most obvious way of implementing this idea is to use menu driven programming. Here a menu appears on the screen from which the user selects the appropriate action. In response to this the menu program then loads the required program and executes it. Once this program is finished control is passed back to the menu program which should display the menu again allowing the user to take any further action.

In terms of the TV Rental Programs the menu could be

```
TV RENTAL SYSTEM
          ------------------------------

     1 Set up new customer file

     2 Change existing customer record

     3 Add new customer records

     4 Delete existing customer records

     5 Print customer bills

     6 Display a customer record

     7 Exit

Enter required option number (1 to 7) -
```

10.1 Executing One Program From Another

In order to carry out the users requirements a particular program will require to be executed. For example, if the TV Rental file is to be set up then that program has to be executed. This program must previously have been compiled with the compiled version being held in a file. It is this compiled version that is called up and executed by the menu program.

If the TV Rental File Set-up Program has been compiled into a file called TVFSUP2.EXE then the C statement to load it and execute it from another program is

```
spawnvp(0, "tvfsup2.exe", argv);
```

The general syntax of this statement is

```
spawnvp(<mode>, <file_name>, <array_of_pointers>);
```

where

<mode> is dependent upon your particular version of C (see your manual).

<file_name> is the name of the file that contains the compiled version of the program to be executed.

<array_of_pointers> is the name of an array which contains pointers to the information that is to be passed to the program.

If the compiled versions of the TV Rental Program suite are held in the following files

File Set-up	is in	TVFSUP2.EXE
File Additions		TVFADD2.EXE
File Deletions		TVFDEL2.EXE
File Amendments		TVFALT2.EXE
File processing		TV19.EXE
Display record		TVFREC2.EXE

then a suitable menu program is given below. A delay() function is included to give the user time to read the screen before the menu is displayed again.

```
#include <stdio.h>

/*TV Rental System Menu Driven - Version 1*/

main(argc,argv)
/*File name specified as a command line argument*/
```

```
int argc;
char *argv[];
{
   int option;

   do
   {
      /*Display menu*/
      display_menu();

      /*Input users requirements*/
      option = user_selection();

      /*Initiate appropriate program or exit*/
      if (option != 7)  /*Exit*/
        call_program(option, argv);
   }
   while (option != 7);   /*Exit*/
}

display_menu()      /*Display menu listing possible options*/
{
   /*Diplay sceen*/
   system("cls");

   /*Output menu*/
   printf("\n            TV RENTAL SYSTEM");
   printf("\n            ----------------");
   printf("\n\n     1  Set up new customer file");
   printf("\n\n     2  Change existing customer record");
   printf("\n\n     3  Add new customer records");
   printf("\n\n     4  Delete existing customer records");
   printf("\n\n     5  Print customer bills");
   printf("\n\n     6  Display a customer record");
   printf("\n\n     7  Exit");
}

user_selection()     /*Input users requirements*/
{
   int opt;

   printf("\n\nEnter required option number (1 to 7) -  ");
   scanf("%d", &opt);
   return(opt);
```

```
}

call_program(opt,argv)      /*Initiate users requirements*/
int opt;
char *argv[];
{
    switch(opt)
    {
      case 1:/*Set up new customer file*/
          spawnvp(0, "tvfsup2.exe", argv);

          /*Produce a delay for user to read screen*/
          delay();
          break;

      case 2:/*Change existing customer record*/
          spawnvp(0, "tvfalt2.exe", argv);

          /*Produce a delay for user to read screen*/
          delay();
          break;

      case 3:/*Add new customer records*/
          spawnvp(0, "tvfadd2.exe", argv);

          /*Produce a delay for user to read screen*/
          delay();
          break;

      case 4:/*Delete existing customer records*/
          spawnvp(0, "tvfdel2.exe", argv);

          /*Produce a delay for user to read screen*/
          delay();
          break;

      case 5:/*Print customer bills*/
          spawnvp(0, "tv19.exe", argv);

          /*Produce a delay for user to read screen*/
          delay();
          break;

      case 6:/*Display a customer record*/
```

```
            spawnvp(0, "tvdrec2.exe", argv);

            /*Produce a delay for user to read screen*/
            delay();
            break;

        default:/*Incorrect input*/
            printf("\nINCORRECT INPUT - ");
            printf("Only options 1 to 7 are allowed\n");

            /*Produce a delay for user to read screen*/
            delay();
        }
}

delay()       /*Introduce delay for user to read screen before
returning to menu*/
{
    int i;
    for (i=0; i <= 20000; ++i);
}
```

If the compiled version of the menu program is held in the file TV and the data file to be used is called CUSTOMER then the statement

```
TV CUSTOMER
```

will start the menu program running. The use of command line arguments will allow the data file name to be passed to all the other programs when required.

10.2 Programming Exercises

1. Convert the mailing list programs from section 9.5 question 2, to a menu driven application program.

11 Directing Output To The Printer

Until now all the output from our programs has been displayed on the screen. It is more likely with application programs that the output is required on a printer rather than a screen. In the C programming language the printer is treated as if it is a file with a special name **prn**.

Therefore, as with any other file, it is necessary to declare a pointer to this file. The user may use any variable name for this pointer. If the pointer is to be prt then the appropriate declaration is

```
FILE *fopen(), *prt;
```

The printer file then has to be opened, for example

```
if ((prt = fopen("prn", "w")) == NULL)
  {
  printf("\n\nCannot open file for printer output\n");
  printf("PROGRAM IS TERMINATED");
  exit();
  }
```

In order to output to the printer file the function **printf()** has to be replaced by the function **fprintf()**.

Like all files once we have finished using the printer the printer file must be closed.

The TV Rental Program converted to send the customer bills and summary table to the printer rather than the screen is given below. Note that the pointer to the printer file is passed to the functions print_bill() and summary(). This is because the printer file is **opened** in main(). Within these functions the pointer must be declared as being of type **FILE**.

```
#include <stdio.h>

/* TV Rental Billing - Version 18
  - Sending output to printer*/
```

```
struct customer_record    /*Defining a customer record*/
     {
     int customer_no;
     int no_of_weeks;
     char tv_type;
     };

main(argc,argv)
/*Passing file name through command line arguments*/
int argc;
char *argv[];
{
    struct customer_record customer;
    int rent_out;
    float rent_per_week, rent_due, weeks_rental();

    /*Declare fp_rent and fp_summ as a file pointers
      and prt as pointer to printer output file*/
    FILE *fopen(), *fp_rent, *fp_summ, *prt;

    /*Open files - rental for reading and summ for writing*/
    if ((fp_rent = fopen(argv[1], "r")) = = NULL)
      {
      printf("\n\nCannot open file %s for reading\n", argv[1]);
      printf("PROGRAM IS TERMINATED");
      exit();
      }

    if ((fp_summ = fopen("summ", "w")) = = NULL)
      {
      printf("\n\nCannot open file 'summ' for writing\n");
      printf("PROGRAM IS TERMINATED");
      exit();
      }

    /*Open printer file for output*/
    if ((prt = fopen("prn", "w")) = = NULL)
      {
      printf("\n\nCannot open file for printer output\n");
      printf("PROGRAM IS TERMINATED");
      exit();
      }

    /*Process customers bills*/
```

```
    do
      {
      /*Input customer record*/
      fscanf(fp_rent, "%4d%2d%c\n", &customer.customer_no,
                  &customer.no_of_weeks, &customer.tv_type);

      /*if end of file customer number is 9999*/
      if (customer.customer_no != 9999)
        {
        /*Determine rent due*/
        rent_per_week = weeks_rental(&customer, &rent_due);

        /*Converting rent_due to integer ready for outputto
          the file. At this stage rounding errors may occur,
          hence the addition of 0.005*/
        rent_out = (rent_due + 0.005) * 100;

        /*Output information to summary file - summ*/
        fprintf(fp_summ, "%4d%2d%c%6d\n", customer, rent_out);

        /*Print the bill*/
        if (rent_per_week != 0)
          print_bill(&customer, rent_per_week, rent_due, prt);
        }
      }
    while(customer.customer_no != 9999);

    /*Output end of file record to file summ*/
    fprintf(fp_summ, "%4d%2d%c%6d\n", 9999, 99, ' ', 9999);

    /*Close files*/
    fclose(fp_rent);
    fclose(fp_summ);

    /*Calculate and output summary table*/
    summary(prt);

    /*Close printer file*/
    fclose(prt);
}

float weeks_rental(cust,due)          /*Determine rent per week*/
struct customer_record *cust;
float *due;
```

```
{
    /*Rent per week*/
    switch ((*cust).tv_type)
    {
    case 'c': /*Colour TV rental is 3.60*/
            *due = (*cust).no_of_weeks*3.60;
            return(3.60);
    case 'b': /*Black and white TV rental is 1.75*/
            *due = (*cust).no_of_weeks*1.75;
            return(1.75);
    case 'v': /*Video rental is 1.50*/
            *due = (*cust).no_of_weeks*1.50;
            return(1.50);
    default : /*Illegal input for tv_type*/
            printf("\n\nProgram does not handle this type of rental\n\n");
            return(0);
    }
}

print_bill(cust, rent, due, prt)      /*Calculate and print the bill*/
struct customer_record *cust;
float rent, due;
FILE *prt;
{
    fprintf(prt, "\n\nTV RENTAL BILL");
    fprintf(prt, "\n\nCustomer number is %d", (*cust).customer_no);
    fprintf(prt, "\nNumber of weeks rent due is %d", (*cust).no_of_weeks);
    fprintf(prt, "\nRent per week is %.2f", rent);
    fprintf(prt, "\n\nRental due is %.2f\n\n", due);
}

summary(prt)     /*Produce summary report*/
FILE *prt;
{
    struct customer_record cust;
    float total, rent_due;
    int rent;

    FILE  *fp_summ;  /*Declare fp_summ as a file pointer*/

    total = 0;    /*Initialise total*/

    /*Open file - summ for reading*/
    if ((fp_summ = fopen("summ", "r")) = = NULL)
```

```
    {
    printf("\n\nCannot open file 'summ' for reading\n");
    printf("PROGRAM IS TERMINATED");
    exit();
    }

  /*Print table headings*/
  fprintf(prt, "\n\n              SUMMARY REPORT");
  fprintf(prt, "\n              ---------------");
  fprintf(prt, "\n\nCustomer number  Weeks due  Rental type  Rent due");
  fprintf(prt, "\n--------------- --------- ----------- --------");

  /*Output summary table*/
  do
    {
    /*Read customer information from file summ*/
    fscanf(fp_summ ,"%4d%2d%c%6d\n", &cust.customer_no,
                   &cust.no_of_weeks, &cust.tv_type, &rent);

    /*If end of file customer number is 9999*/
    if (cust.customer_no ! = 9999)
      {
      /*Print table of customer information*/

      /*Rent due was written to the file as an integer
        therefore has to be converted back to a floating
        point number*/
      rent_due = rent / 100.0;

      fprintf(prt,"\n    %4d        %2d        %c       %6.2f",
                                  cust, rent_due);

      /*Calculate total rent due*/
      total = total + rent_due;
      }
    }
  while (cust.customer_no ! = 9999);
  /*Close file*/
  fclose(fp_summ);

  /*Print total rent due*/
  fprintf(prt,"\n\n              Total rent due is %12.2f\n\n", total);
}
```

Appendix A
Keywords In C

The following are reserved for keywords in the C programming language and may not be used as identifiers:

auto	extern	sizeof
break	float	static
case	for	struct
char	goto	switch
continue	if	typedef
default	int	union
do	long	unsigned
double	register	while
else	return	
entry	short	

Appendix B
Table Of ASCII Codes

ASCII	Char	ASCII	Char	ASCII	Char	ASCII	Char	ASCII	Char
0	NUL	26	SUB	52	4	78	N	104	h
1	SOH	27	ESC	53	5	79	O	105	i
2	STX	28	FS	54	6	80	P	106	j
3	ETX	29	GS	55	7	81	Q	107	k
4	EOT	30	HOME	56	8	82	R	108	l
5	ENQ	31	NL	57	9	83	S	109	m
6	ACK	32	SPACE	58	:	84	T	110	n
7	BEL	33	!	59	;	85	U	111	o
8	B$	34	"	60	<	86	V	112	p
9	SKIP	35	#	61	=	87	W	113	q
10	LF	36	$	62	>	88	X	114	r
11	VT	37	%	63	?	89	Y	115	s
12	FF	38	&	64	@	90	Z	116	t
13	CR	39	'	65	A	91	[	117	u
14	SO	40	(	66	B	92	\	118	v
15	SI	41	)	67	C	93	]	119	w
16	DLE	42	*	68	D	94	^	120	x
17	DC1	43	+	69	E	95	_	121	y
18	DC2	44	,	70	F	96	`	122	z
19	DC3	45	-	71	G	97	a	123	{
20	DC4	46	.	72	H	98	b	124	|
21	NAK	47	/	73	I	99	c	125	}
22	SYN	48	0	74	J	100	d	126	~
23	ETB	49	1	75	K	101	e	127	DEL
24	CAN	50	2	76	L	102	f		
25	EM	51	3	77	M	103	g		

Appendix C
Solutions To Programming Exercises

Programming Exercises 1.4

```
#include <stdio.h>
/*Programming exercise 1.4.1 - Print name and address*/

main()
{
    /*Name and address output on one line*/
    printf("\nJoe Bloggs  The Temple Building  ");
    printf("12 High Street  Old Town  OT1 2BE");

    /*Name and address output as on an envelope*/
    printf("\n\n\nJoe Bloggs\nThe Temple Building");
    printf("\n12 High Street\nOld Town\nOT1 2BE");
}
```

```
Joe Bloggs  The Temple Building  12 High Street  Old Town  OT1 2BE

Joe Bloggs
The Temple Building
12 High Street
Old Town
OT1 2BE
```

```
#include <stdio.h>
/*Programming exercise 1.4.2 -  Convert temperature in Celsius to
                    Fahrenheit                    */

main()
{
```

```
    int celsius;
    float fahrenheit;

    /*Input temperature in Celsius*/
    printf("\nEnter degees Celsius ");
    scanf("%3d",&celsius);

    /*Calculate Fahrenheit equivalent*/
    fahrenheit = 32+celsius*(9.0/5); /*Righthand side must result in float*/

    /*Output temperature conversion*/
    printf("\n\n%d Celsius is %f Fahrenheit\n\n",celsius,fahrenheit);
}
```

Enter degrees Celsius **20**

20 Celsius is 68.00 Fahrenheit

```
#include <stdio.h>
/*Programming exercise 1.4.3 - Area and perimeter of a rectangle*/

main()
{
    int length, breadth;
    float area, perimeter;

    /*Input length and breadth of rectangle*/
    printf("\n\nEnter the length of the rectangle in feet ");
    scanf("%3d", &length);
    printf("\nEnter the breadth of the rectangle in feet ");
    scanf("%3d", &breadth);

    /*Calculate area in square yards*/
    area = (length * breadth)/9.0;

    /*Calculate perimeter in yards*/
    perimeter = 2 * (length + breadth)/3.0;

    /*Output area and perimeter*/
    printf("\n\nA rectangle %d ft in length and %d ft in breadth has an ",
                                            length, breadth);
    printf("\narea of %f square yards and a", area);
    printf("\nperimeter of %f yards\n\n\n", perimeter);
```

```
}
```

Enter the length of the rectangle in feet **6**
Enter the breadth of the rectangle in feet **3**

A rectangle 6 ft in length and 3 ft in breadth has an
area of 2.000000 square yards and a
perimeter of 6.000000 yards

Programming Exercises 2.3

```
/*Programming exercise 2.3.1 - Functions for performing arithmetic
                  operations on two numbers*/

add(a,b)      /*Adding two numbers a + b*/
int a,b;
{
   return(a + b);
}

subtract(a,b) /*Subtracting two numbers a - b*/
int a,b;
{
   return(a - b);
}

multiply(a,b) /*Multiplying two numbers a x b*/
int a,b;
{
   return(a * b);
}

float divide(a,b)    /*Division of two numbers a divided by b*/
int a,b;
{
   return(a * 1.0 / b);  /*1.0 gives a decimal result rather
                  than an integer one        */
}
```

```
#include <stdio.h>
/*Programming exercise 2.3.2 - Arithmetic operations on two numbers*/

main()
{
    int num_1, num_2;
    float divide();

    /*Input two numbers*/
    printf("\nEnter first number ");
    scanf("%d",&num_1);
    printf("\nEnter second number ");
    scanf("%d",&num_2);

    /*Output arithmetic calculations*/
    printf("\n\n%d + %d = %d", num_1, num_2, add(num_1,num_2));
    printf("\n\n%d - %d = %d", num_1, num_2, subtract(num_1,num_2));
    printf("\n\n%d x %d = %d", num_1, num_2, multiply(num_1,num_2));
    printf("\n\n%d divided by %d = %f\n",num_1, num_2,
divide(num_1,num_2));
}

add(a,b)      /*Adding two numbers a + b*/
int a,b;
{
    return(a + b);
}

subtract(a,b)  /*Subtracting two numbers a - b*/
int a,b;
{
    return(a - b);
}

multiply(a,b)  /*Multiplying two numbers a x b*/
int a,b;
{
    return(a * b);
}

float divide(a,b)    /*Division of two numbers a divided by b*/
int a,b;
{
```

```
    return(a * 1.0 / b);  /*1.0 gives a decimal result rather
                          than an integer one           */
}
```

Enter first number **60**

Enter second number **30**

60 + 30 = 90

60 - 30 = 30

60 x 30 = 1800

60 divided by 30 = 2.000000

```
#include <stdio.h>
/*Programming exercise 2.3.3 - ASCII equivalent of a character*/

main()
{
    int character;

    /*Input a character*/
    printf("\nEnter a character ");
    scanf("%s",&character);

    /*Determine and output ASCII equivalent of character*/
    char_ascii(character);
}

char_ascii(character)   /*Character to ASCII conversion*/
int character;
{
    /*Output ASCII equivalent*/
    printf("\nThe ASCII for %c is %d",character, character);
}
```

Enter a character **A**

The ASCII for A is 65

Programming Exercises 3.4

```
#include <stdio.h>
/*Programming exercise 3.4.1 - Number a multiple of 3*/

main()
{
    int number;

    /*Input number*/
    printf("\nEnter a whole number ");
    scanf("%d", &number);

    /*Is number a multiple of 3*/
    multiple_3(number);
}

multiple_3(num)      /*Determines whether num is multiple of 3*/
int num;
{
    printf("\nThe number %d is ", num);
    if ((num % 3) == 0)  /*ie no remainder*/
      printf("divisible by 3\n\n");
    else
      printf("not divisible by 3\n\n");
}
```

Enter a whole number **60**
The number is divisible by 3

Enter a whole number **83**
The number is not divisible by 3

```
#include <stdio.h>
/*Programming exercise 3.4.2 - Temperature conversion*/

main()
{
    int temperature;
    char degrees;

    /*Input temperature*/
```

```
    printf("\nEnter a temperature ");
    scanf("%d", &temperature);

    /*Input temperature scale*/
    printf("Enter c if temperature is in degrees celsius");
    printf("\n     f if temperature is in degrees fahrenheit  ");
    scanf("%s", &degrees);

    /*Temperature conversion*/
    if (degrees = = 'c')
      cel_fah(temperature);
    else
      fah_cel(temperature);
}

cel_fah(temp)       /*Celsius to fahrenheit conversion*/
int temp;
{
    float fahrenheit;
    fahrenheit = temp * (9.0 / 5) + 32;
    printf("\n%d degrees Celsius is %.2f degrees Fahrenheit",
                                    temp, fahrenheit);
}

fah_cel(temp)       /*Fahrenheit to celsius conversion*/
int temp;
{
    float celsius;
    celsius = (5 / 9.0) * (temp - 32);
    printf("\n%d degrees Fahrenheit is %.2f degrees Celsius",
                                    temp, celsius);
}
```

Enter a temperature **20**
Enter c if temperature is in degrees celsius
        f if temperature is in degrees fahrenheit **c**

20 degrees Celsius is 68.00 degrees Fahrenheit

Enter a temperature **32**
Enter c if temperature is in degrees celsius
        f if temperature is in degrees fahrenheit **f**

32 degrees Fahrenheit is 0.00 degrees Celsius

```
#include <stdio.h>
/*Programming exercise 3.4.3 - Checking for non-numeric character*/

main()
{
    int character;

    /*Input a character*/
    printf("\nEnter a single character  ");
    scanf("%d", &character);

    /*Checking that character input was a numeric digit*/
    numeric(character);
}

numeric(num)    /*Checking that num is a numeric digit*/
int num;
{
    if (num >= 0 && num <= 9)
      printf("\nInput character is the number %d", num);
    else
      printf("\nInput character is not a number");
}
```

Enter a single character **6**
Input character is the number 6

Enter a single character **g**
Input character is not a number

Programming Exercises 3.7

```
#include <stdio.h>
/*Programming exercise 3.7.1  -  Menu selection of arithmetic
                               operations              */

main()
{
    int number_1, number_2, menu_option;

    /*Input 2 integer values less than 10*/
    printf("\nEnter first number  ");
```

```
    scanf("%d", &number_1);
    printf("Enter second number  ");
    scanf("%d", &number_2);

    /*Select arithmetic operation from menu*/
    menu_option = menu();

    /*Perform arithmetic operation for a valid menu option */
    if (menu_option > = 0 && menu_option < = 5)  /*Valid option*/
      arith_operation(menu_option, number_1, number_2);
    else
      {
        printf("\nInvalid choice. Option should be in the ");
      printf("range 1 to 5\nPROGRAM TERMINATED");
      }
}

menu()            /*Outputs a menu and inputs selected option*/
{
     int selection;

    /*Output menu*/
    printf("\n\n1  Total two numbers");
    printf("\n\n2  Subtract one number from the other");
    printf("\n\n3  Multiply one number by the other");
    printf("\n\n4  Divide one number by the other");
    printf("\n\n5  None of the above");

    /*Input users selection*/
    printf("\n\n\nWhich of the above options is required?");
    printf("\nEnter a number between 1 and 5  ");
    scanf("%d", &selection);

    return(selection);
}

arith_operation(option, no_1, no_2)  /*Performing required arithmetic
                                       operation*/
int option, no_1, no_2;
{
    switch(option)
    {
    case 1:/*Addition*/
          printf("\n%d + %d = %d", no_1, no_2, no_1 + no_2);
```

```
        break;
    case 2:/*Subtraction*/
        printf("\n%d - %d = %d", no_1, no_2, no_1 - no_2);
        break;
    case 3:/*Multiplication*/
        printf("\n%d x %d = %d", no_1, no_2, no_1 * no_2);
        break;
    case 4:/*Division  nb 1.0 converts to overcome integer division*/
        printf("\n%d / %d = %f", no_1, no_2, no_1 * 1.0 / no_2);
        break;
    case 5:/*None of the above*/
        printf("\nNone of the arithmetic functions required");
        break;
    }

}
```

Enter first number **30**
Enter second number **50**

1 Total two numbers

2 Subtract one number from the other

3 Multiply one number by the other

4 Divide one number by the other

5 None of the above

Which of the above options is required?
Enter a number between 1 and 5 **1**

30 + 50 = 80

Enter first number **40**
Enter second number **60**

1 Total two numbers

2 Subtract one number from the other

3 Multiply one number by the other

4 Divide one number by the other

5 None of the above

Which of the above options is required?
Enter a number between 1 and 5 **2**

40 + 60 = -20

Enter first number **30**
Enter second number **60**

1 Total two numbers

2 Subtract one number from the other

3 Multiply one number by the other

4 Divide one number by the other

5 None of the above

Which of the above options is required?
Enter a number between 1 and 5 **3**

30 * 50 = 180

Enter first number **40**
Enter second number **30**

1 Total two numbers

2 Subtract one number from the other

3 Multiply one number by the other

4 Divide one number by the other

5 None of the above

Which of the above options is required?
Enter a number between 1 and 5 **4**

40 / 30 = 1.333333

Enter first number **40**
Enter second number **10**

1 Total two numbers

2 Subtract one number from the other

3 Multiply one number by the other

4 Divide one number by the other

5 None of the above

Which of the above options is required?
Enter a number between 1 and 5 **5**

None of the arithmetic functions required

Enter first number **40**
Enter second number **20**

1 Total two numbers

2 Subtract one number from the other

3 Multiply one number by the other

4 Divide one number by the other

5 None of the above

Which of the above options is required?

```
Enter a number between 1 and 5  8

Invalid choice.  Option should be in the range 1 to 5
PROGRAM TERMINATED
```

```
/*Programming exercise 3.7.2  -  Lookup table for quantity discounts*/


look_up(quantity)        /*Determine quantity discount*/
int quantity;
{
    switch(quantity)
    {
    case 1:/*Quantity 1 - 0% discount*/
        return(0);
    case 2:/*Quantity 2 to 4 - 5% discount*/
    case 3:
    case 4:
        return(5);
    default:/*Quantity 5 or more - 10% discount*/
        return(10);
    }
}
```

```
#include<stdio.h>
/*Programming exercise 3.7.3  -  Quantity discounts*/

main()
{
    int cost, number_bought, discount;
    float total_cost;

    /*Input cost of item - single digit integer*/
    printf("\nEnter the cost of the item  ");
    scanf("%d", &cost);

    /*Input number of items bought - single digit integer*/
    printf("Enter the number of items bought  ");
    scanf("%d", &number_bought);

    /*Determine quantity discount*/
    discount = look_up(number_bought);
```

```
    /*Calculate and print bill*/
    total_cost = (number_bought * cost) * (1 - discount / 100.0);
    printf("\nCost of goods is %.2f with a discount of %2d%%",
                                total_cost, discount);
}

look_up(quantity)       /*Determine quantity discount*/
int quantity;
{
    switch(quantity)
    {
    case 1:/*Quantity 1 - 0% discount*/
        return(0);
    case 2:/*Quantity 2 to 4 - 5% discount*/
    case 3:
    case 4:
        return(5);
    default:/*Quantity 5 or more - 10% discount*/
        return(10);
    }
}
```

Enter the cost of the item **10**
Enter the number of items bought **3**

Cost of goods is 28.50 with a discount of 5%

Enter the cost of the item **20**
Enter the number of items bought **1**

Cost of goods is 20.00 with a discount of 0%

Enter the cost of the item **50**
Enter the number of items bought **6**

Cost of goods is 270.00 with a discount of 10%

Programming Exercises 4.6

```
#include <stdio.h>
/*Programming exercise 4.6.1 - Output a number of 'Hello there!'s */
```

```
main()
{
   int number,i;

   /*Input a single digit integer*/
   printf("\nHow many "Hello there!'s" are to be output  ");
   scanf("%d", &number);

   /*Output the required number of 'Hello there!'s*/
   printf("\nHello there! will be output %d times\n", number);
   for (i=1; i< =number; i+ +)
      printf("\nHello there!");
}
```

```
How many "Hello there!'s" are to be output  3

Hello there! will be output 3 times

Hello there!
Hello there!
Hello there!
```

```
#include <stdio.h>

/*Programming exercise4.6.2 - Temperature conversion table*/

main()
{
   int i;

   /*Output table headings*/
   printf("\n\nCelsius  Fahrenheit");

   /*Output conversion table*/
   for (i=0; i< =30; i+ +);
      printf("\n%4d     %6.2f", i, i * (9 / 5.0) + 32);
}
```

```
Celsius  Fahrenheit
    0       32.00
    1       33.80
    2       35.60
    3       37.40
```

```
 4    39.20
 5    41.00
 6    42.80
 7    44.60
 8    46.40
 9    48.20
10    50.00
11    51.80
12    53.60
13    55.40
14    57.20
15    59.00
16    60.80
17    62.60
18    64.40
19    66.20
20    68.00
21    69.80
22    71.60
23    73.40
24    75.20
25    77.00
26    78.80
27    80.60
28    82.40
29    84.20
30    86.00
```

```
#include <stdio.h>
/*Programming exercise 4.6.3 - x to the power of n*/

main()
{
    int number, power_of;
    char another_no;

    do
      {
      /*Input number and power of*/
      printf("\nEnter a number ");
      scanf("%d", &number);
      printf("to be raised to the power of ");
      scanf("%d", &power_of);
```

```
        /*Calculate and output number to the power of*/
        printf("\n%d to the power of %d is %d\n", number,
                        power_of, power(number, power_of));

        /*Calculations to be repeated*/
        printf("\nDo you want to calculate another power (y or n)  ");
        scanf("%s", &another_no);
        }
    while(another_no = = 'y');
}

power(x, n)              /*Raise x to the power of n*/
int x, n;
{
    int i, result;

    /*Power of 0*/
    if (n = = 0)
      return(1);

    /*Power of 1*/
    if (n = = 1)
      return(x);

    /*Other powers*/
    result = x;
    for (i=1; i < n; i+ +)
       result = result * x;
    return(result);
}
```

```
Enter a number 30
to be raised to the power of 0

30 to the power of 0 is 1

Do you want to calculate another power (y or n) y


Enter a number 2
to be raised to the power of 1

2 to the power of 1 is 2
```

Do you want to calculate another power (y or n) **y**

Enter a number **4**
to be raised to the power of **2**

4 to the power of 2 is 16

Do you want to calculate another power (y or n) **y**

Enter a number **3**
to be raised to the power of **5**

3 to the power of 5 is 243

Do you want to calculate another power (y or n) **n**

Programming Exercises 5.3

```
#include <stdio.h>
/*Programming exercise 5.3.1 - Sorting two integers into ascending order*/

main()
{
    int no_1, no_2;
    char more;

    do
      {
      /*Input two numbers*/
      printf("\nEnter two whole numbers (separated by a space) ");
      scanf("%d %d", &no_1, &no_2);

      /*Arrange numbers in ascending order*/
      order(&no_1, &no_2);

      /*Print ordered list*/
      printf("\nNumbers in ascending order are %d %d");

      /*More pairs of numbers*/
      printf("\n\nMore pairs of numbers to be ordered (y or n)? ");
      scanf("%s", &more);
      }
```

```
    while(more = = 'y');
}

order(n1,n2)      /*Sort numbers into ascending order*/
int *n1, *n2;
{
    int temp;
    if (*n1 > *n2)
      {
      temp = *n1;
      *n1 = *n2;
      *n2 = temp;
      }
}
```

Enter two whole numbers (separated by a space) **40 60**

Numbers in ascending order are 40 60

More pairs of numbers to be ordered (y or n)? **y**

Enter two whole numbers (separated by a space) **50 15**

Numbers in ascending order are 15 50

More pairs of numbers to be ordered (y or n)? **y**

Enter two whole numbers (separated by a space) **20 20**

Numbers in ascending order are 20 20

More pairs of numbers to be ordered (y or n)? **n**

```
#include <stdio.h>
/*Programming exercise 5.3.2 - Conversion of metres to yards, feet
                     and inches                  */
main()
{
    int yds, ft, ins;
    float metres;

    /*Input material length in metres*/
    printf("\n\nEnter the amount of material required in metres  ");
```

```
    scanf("%f", &metres);

    /*Convert metres to yards feet and inches*/
    metre_con(metres, &yds, &ft, &ins);

    /*Output conversion*/
    printf("\n%.2f metres is %d yds %d ft %d ins\n\n",
                                metres, yds, ft, ins);
}

metre_con(m,y,f,i)        /*Metres to yards, feet and inches*/
float m;
int *y, *f, *i;
{
    m = m * 100 / 2.54;     /*Metres converted to inches*/
    *y = m / 36;
    m = m - (*y) * 36;      /*Inches remaining after yards*/
    *f = m / 12;
    *i = m - (*f) * 12;     /*Remaining feet*/
}
```

```
Enter the amount of material required in metres  1

1.00 metres is 1 yds 0 ft 3 ins
```

```
#include <stdio.h>
/*Programming example 5.3.3  -  Simple payroll*/

main()
{
    int employee_no, no_hrs_worked;
    float pay, calc_pay(), rate_of_pay;
    char week_or_hour, another_payslip;

    do
    {
      /*Input employee details*/
      employee_input(&employee_no, &no_hrs_worked, &rate_of_pay,
                                   &week_or_hour);

      /*Calculate weeks salary*/
      pay = calc_pay(no_hrs_worked, rate_of_pay, week_or_hour);
```

```
        /*Output payslip*/
        payslip(employee_no, no_hrs_worked, rate_of_pay, week_or_hour,
pay);

        /*Monetary denominations required for pay*/
        cash(pay);

        /*Another payslip to compute?*/
        printf("\nMore payslips to be calculated (y or n)? ");
        scanf("%s", &another_payslip);
    }
    while (another_payslip = = 'y');
}

employee_input(emp_no,hrs,rate,w_h)   /*Input employee details*/
int *emp_no, *hrs, *rate;
char *w_h;
{
    printf("\nEnter employee number ");
    scanf("%d",emp_no);
    rintf("Is employee paid by the hour (y or n)? ");
    scanf("%s", w_h);
    if (*w_h = = 'y')

        {           /*Paid by hour*/
        *w_h = 'h';
        printf("How many hours worked? ");
        scanf("%d", hrs);
        printf("Rate of pay per hour ");
        scanf("%f", rate);
        }

    else
        {           /*Paid weekly wage*/
        *w_h = 'w';
        printf("Enter weekly wage ");
        scanf("%f", rate);
        }
}

float calc_pay(hrs,rate,w_h)          /*Calculate pay*/
int hrs;
float rate;
char w_h;
```

```
{
    if (w_h = = 'h')
      return(hrs * rate);      /*Paid hourly*/
    else
      return(rate);            /*Paid weekly wages*/
}

payslip(emp_no,hrs,rate,w_h,wages)       /*Print wage slip*/
int emp_no, hrs;
float rate, wages;
char w_h;
{
    printf("\n\nEmployee number %d", emp_no);
    if (w_h = = 'w')
      printf("\nWeeks earnings are %.2f", wages);
    else
      {
      printf("\nRate of pay per hour is %.2f", rate);
      printf("\nNumber of hours worked is %d", hrs);
      printf("\n\nWeeks earnings are %.2f", wages);
      }
}

cash(wages)       /*Determine monetary values required to make up wages*/
float wages;
{
    int pound_20, pound_10, pound_5, pound_1, pence_50, pence_20,
       pence_10, pence_5, pence_2, pence_1, pounds, pence;

    pounds = wages;
    pence = (wages - pounds) * 100 + 0.01; /*0.01 compensates for
                                            rounding to 2 decimal places*/

    pound_20 = pounds / 20;             /*No. 20 notes*/
    pounds = pounds - pound_20 * 20;    /*Remaining wages*/
    pound_10 = pounds / 10;             /*No. 10 notes*/
    pounds = pounds - pound_10 * 10;    /*Remaining wages*/
    pound_5 = pounds / 5;               /*No. 5 notes*/
    pounds = pounds - pound_5 * 5;      /*Remaining wages*/
    pound_1 = pounds;                   /*No. 1 notes*/
    pounds = pounds - pound_1;          /*Remaining wages*/
    pence_50 = pence / 50;              /*No. 50p coins*/
    pence = pence - pence_50 * 50;      /*Remaining wages*/
    pence_20 = pence / 20;              /*No. 20p coins*/
```

```
    pence = pence - pence_20 * 20;      /*Remaining wages*/
    pence_10 = pence / 10;              /*No. 10p coins*/
    pence = pence - pence_10 * 10;      /*Remaining wages*/
    pence_5 = pence / 5;                /*No. 5p coins*/
    pence = pence - pence_5 * 5;        /*Remaining wages*/
    pence_2 = pence / 2;                /*No. 2p coins*/
    pence = pence - pence_2 * 2;        /*Remaining wages*/
    pence_1 = pence;                    /*No. 1p coins*/

    /*Output makeup of wages*/
    printf("\n\nThe weeks wages will be made up with - ");
    printf("\n\n 20  10  5  1 50p 20p 10p 5p 2p 1p");
    printf("\n %2d %2d %2d %2d %2d %2d %2d %2d %2d
                                                  %2d\n\n",
        pound_20, pound_10, pound_5, pound_1, pence_50, pence_20,
        pence_10, pence_5, pence_2, pence_1);
}
```

Enter employee number **4444**
Is employee paid by the hour (y or n)? **n**
Enter weekly wage **128**

Employee number 4444
Weeks earnings are 128.00

The weeks wages will be made up with -

```
20 10  5  1 50p 20p 10p 5p 2p 1p
 6  0  1  3  0   0   0  0  0  0
```

More payslips to be calculated (y or n)? **y**

Enter employee number **5555**
Is employee paid by the hour (y or n)? **y**
How many hours worked? **40**
Rate of pay per hour **3.56**

Employee number 5555
Rate of pay per hour is 3.56
Number of hours worked is 40

Weeks earnings are 142.40

The weeks wages will be made up with -

```
20  10  5  1  50p 20p 10p  5p  2p  1p
 7   0  0  2   0   2    0   0   0   0
```

More payslips to be calculated (y or n)? **n**

Programming Exercises 6.1

```
#include <stdio.h>
/*Programming exercise 6.1.1 - Calculate average of a series of numbers*/

main()
{
    int no_numbers;
    float number[100], average, ave();

    /*Input list of numbers*/
    input_nos(&no_numbers, number);

    /*Calculate average*/
    average = ave(no_numbers, number);

    /*Output the list of numbers and their average*/
    print_nos(number, average, no_numbers);
}

input_nos(count,nos)     /*Input list of numners*/
int *count;
float *nos;
{
    char another_no;
    *count = 0;
    do
    {
      /*Input a number*/
      ++(*count);
      printf("Enter a number  ");
      scanf("%f", &nos[*count]);
```

```
        if (*count < 100)          /*Storage for maximum of 100 numbers*/
          {
          /*Another number?*/
          printf("More numbers (y or n)?  ");
          scanf("%s", &another_no);
          }
      }
      while(another_no = = 'y' && (*count) < = 101);
}

float ave(count, nos)          /*Return average of list of numbers*/
int count;
float *nos;
{
    int i;
    float total;
    total = 0;

    /*Total list of numbers*/
    for (i=1; i< =count; i+ +)
       total = total + nos[i];

    /*Return average*/
    return(total / count);
}

print_nos(nos,average,count)     /*Output list of numbers and their average*/
int count;
float *nos, average;
{
    int i;

    printf("\nThe following list of numbers\n");

    /*Output list of numbers*/
    for(i=1; i < = count; i+ +)
       printf("\n%f", nos[i]);

    /*Output average*/
    printf("\n\nhave an average of %f", average);
}
```

```
Enter a number  40
More numbers (y or n)?  y
```

```
Enter a number 30
More numbers (y or n)? y
Enter a number 20
More numbers (y or n)? n

The following list of numbers

40.000000
30.000000
20.000000

have an average of 30.000000
```

```
#include <stdio.h>
/*Programming exercise 6.1.2 - Names*/

main()
{
    char name[50];

    /*Input name*/
    input_name(name);

    /*Output name*/
    output_name(name);

    /*Output name - surname first*/
    surname_christian(name);
}

input_name(nam)             /*Input name*/
char *nam;
{
    int i;
    i = 0;

    printf("\nEnter a name (christian name and surname)\n");
    do
    {
      /*Input a character*/
      ++i;
      nam[i] = getchar();
```

```
        /*Restrict name to 49 characters*/
        if (i = = 50)
            nam[i] = '\n';    /*Carriage return*/
    }
    while(nam[i] ! = '\n');
}

output_name(nam)                /*Output name*/
char *nam;
{
    int i;
    i = 0;
    printf("\n");
    do
    {
        + +i;
        printf("%c", nam[i]);
    }
    while(nam[i] ! = '\n');
}

surname_christian(nam)          /*Reverse surname and christian name*/
char *nam;
{
    int i;
    i = 0;

    /*Looking for space between names*/
    do
        + +i;
    while(nam[i] ! = ' ');

    /*Output surname*/
    printf("\n");
    do
    {
        + +i;
        if (nam[i] ! = '\n')
            printf("%c", nam[i]);
    }
    while(nam[i] ! = '\n');

    /*Output space followed by christian name*/
    printf(" ");
```

```
    i = 0;
    do
    {
       + +i;
       printf("%c", nam[i]);
    }
    while(nam[i] != ' ');
}
```

Enter a name (christian name and surname)
Michael Trotter

Michael Trotter

Trotter Michael

```
#include <stdio.h>
/*Programming exercise 6.1.3 - String conversion*/

main()
{
    char string[100];

    /*Input string*/
    input_string(string);

    /*Convert string to lower case*/
    lower_case(string);

    /*Output string*/
    output_string(string);

    /*Convert string to upper case*/
    capitals(string);

    /*Output string*/
    output_string(string);

    /*Reverse the order of the characters in the string*/
    reverse(string);

    /*Output string*/
    output_string(string);
```

```
}

input_string(str)             /*Input string*/
char *str;
{
    int i;
    i = 0;

    printf("\nEnter a string of characters (less then 100 characters)\n");
    do
    {
      /*Input a character*/
      + +i;
      str[i] = getchar();

      /*Restrict string to 100 characters*/
      if (i = = 100)
        str[i] = '\n';    /*Carriage return*/
    }
    while(str[i] != '\n');
}

output_string(str)              /*Output string*/
char str;
{
    int i;
    i = 0;
    printf("\n");
    do
    {
      + +i;
      printf("%c", str[i]);
    }
    while(str[i] != '\n');
}

lower_case(str)          /*Converts string to lower case characters*/
char *str;
{
    int i;
    i = 0;
    do
    {
      + +i;
```

```
        str[i] = tolower(str[i]);
    }
    while (str[i] ! = '\n');
}

capitals(str)         /*Converts string to upper case characters*/
char *str;
{
    int i;
    i = 0;
    do
    {
        + +i;
        str[i] = toupper(str[i]);
    }
    while (str[i] ! = '\n');
}

reverse(str)          /*Reverse the order of the string*/
char *str;
{
    char rev_str[100];
    int i, j, no_chars;
    no_chars = 0;

    /*Find the end of the string*/
    do
        + +no_chars;
    while (str[no_chars] ! = '\n');

    /*Reverse the string*/
    for (i=1, j=no_chars; i< =no_chars; i+ +, j--)
        rev_str[i] = str[j];

    /*Replace reverse string into original string*/
    for (i = 2; i< =no_chars; i+ +)
        str[i-1] = rev_str[i];

    /*Move carriage return to end of string*/
    str[i] = '\n';
}
```

Enter a string of characters (less than 100 characters)
Is it Friday yet?

is it friday yet?

IS IT FRIDAY YET?

?TEY YADIRF TI SI

Programming exercises 7.5

```
#include <stdio.h>
/*Programming exercise 7.5.1 - Goal statistics*/

struct football      /*Defining a structure for a football player*/
    {
    char name[30];
    char team[30];
    int goals;
    };

main()
{
   struct football player[100];
   int option;

   /*Initialise player arry*/
   init_player(player);

   do
   {
     /*Display menu of options*/
     menu();

     /*Determine users requirements*/
     menu_choice(&option);

     /*Perform users specified option*/
     switch(option)
     {
     case 1:/*Enter information on all football players into array*/
         player_input(player);
         break;
     case 2:/*Display table for all footballers*/
         goal_table(player);
```

```
            break;
        case 3:/*Update specific footballers goal tally*/
            goal_update(player);
            break;
        case 4:/*Exit from program*/
            break;
        default:/*Illegal input*/
            printf("\n\nThis is not an available option.");
            printf("\nAvailable options are 1, 2, 3, or 4");
        }
    }
    while(option != 4);
}

init_player(player)      /*Initialises structure - char to spaces and
                                    numbers to 0      */
struct football player[];
{
    nt i, j;
    for (i=0; i<100; ++i)
    {
      for (j=0; j<30; ++j)
      {
        player[i].name[j] = ' ';
        player[i].team[j] = ' ';
      }
      player[i].goals = 0;
    }
}

menu()      /*Display a menu of program options to the user*/
{
    /*Clear screen*/
    system("cls");

    /*Display menu*/
    printf("\n\n        FOOTBALL SYSTEM");
    printf("\n          ______________");
    printf("\n\n1  Enter information on all football players");
    printf("\n\n2  Display table for all footballers");
    printf("\n\n3  Update specific footballers goal tally");
    printf("\n\n4  Exit from program");
```

```
menu_choice(opt)        /*Input users menu selection*/
int *opt;
{
   printf("\n\nSelect one of the above (1 to 4)  ");
   scanf("%d", opt);

   /*Clear screen*/
   system("cls");
}

player_input(player)      /*Enter information on all players into array*/
struct football player[];
{
   int i;
   char more;

   i = -1;
   do
   {
      + +i;

      /*Input players name*/
      printf("Enter players name  ");
      input_string(player[i].name);

      /*Input players team*/
      printf("Enter players team  ");
      input_string(player[i].team);

      /*Input number of goals scored*/
      fflush(stdin);
      printf("Enter number of goals scored  ");
      scanf("%d",& player[i].goals);

      /*More players?*/
      if (i < 99)
        {
        printf("More footballers to be entered (y or n)?  ");
        scanf("%s", &more);
        }
   }
   while(more = = 'y' && i < 99);

   /*Terminate player list*/
```

```
    if (i < 99)
      player[i+1].goals = -1;
}

input_string(alpha)     /*Input a string of up to 31 characters*/
char *alpha;
{
    int i;
    i = -1;

    /*Flush the keyboard buffer*/
    fflush(stdin);

    do
    {
      ++i;

      /*Input a character*/
      alpha[i] = getchar();
    }
    while(alpha[i] != '\n' && i < 29);

    /*Terminate string*/
    alpha[i] = '\0';
}

goal_table(player)      /*Display table of goals scored*/
struct football player[];
{
    int i;
    char cont;

    i = 0;

    /*Output table headings*/
    printf("\n\nName                          ");
    printf("Team                          Goals");
    printf("\n----                          ");
    printf("----                          -----");

    while(player[i].goals != -1 || i > 99)
    {
      /*Output player information*/
      printf("\n%-30s %-30s  %-4d", player[i].name,
```

```
                    player[i].team, player[i].goals);

        ++i;
    }

    printf("\n\nPress C to continue ");
    scanf("%s", &cont);
}

goal_update(player)      /*Update players goal tally*/
struct football player[];
{
    char name[30];
    int i, match, goal;

    /*Input players name to be updated*/
    printf("Enter name of player ");
    input_string(name);

    /*Find players record*/
    i = 0;
    while((player[i].goals != -1) && (i < 100) &&
                (match = strcmp(name, player[i].name) != 0))
        ++i;

    /*Input number of goals to be added*/
    printf("Enter number of goals to be added to players account ");
    scanf("%d", &goal);

    /*Update players record*/
    if (match == 0)
      player[i].goals = player[i].goals + goal;
    else
      printf("\n\nPlayer %s is not in the goal table\n", name);
}
```

FOOTBALL SYSTEM

---

1 Enter information on all football players

2 Display table for all footballers

3 Update specific footballers goal tally

4 Exit from program

Select one of the above (1 to 4) **1**

Enter players name **John Smith**
Enter players team **All Commers**
Enter number of goals scored **2**
Are there more footballers to be entered (y or n) **y**
Enter players name **Fred Bloggs**
Enter players team **United**
Enter number of goals scored **0**
Are there more footballers to be entered (y or n) **y**
Enter players name **Ted Shoe**
Enter players team **United**
Enter number of goals scored **10**
Are there more footballers to be entered (y or n) **n**

FOOTBALL SYSTEM

---

1 Enter information on all football players

2 Display table for all footballers

3 Update specific footballers goal tally

4 Exit from program

Select one of the above (1 to 4) **2**

Name	Team	Goals
-------	-------	-----
John Smith	All Commers	2
Fred Bloggs	United	0
Ted Shoe	United	10

Press C to continue

FOOTBALL SYSTEM

---

1 Enter information on all football players

2 Display table for all footballers

3 Update specific footballers goal tally

4 Exit from program

Select one of the above (1 to 4) **3**

Enter name of player **Fred Bloggs**
Enter number of goals to be added to the players account **3**

FOOTBALL SYSTEM

---

1 Enter information on all football players

2 Display table for all footballers

3 Update specific footballers goal tally

4 Exit from program

Select one of the above (1 to 4) **2**

Name	Team	Goals
---------	-------	-------
John Smith	All Commers	2
Fred Bloggs	United	3
Ted Shoe	United	10

Press C to continue

FOOTBALL SYSTEM

---

1 Enter information on all football players

2 Display table for all footballers

3 Update specific footballers goal tally

4 Exit from program

Select one of the above (1 to 4) **6**

Available options are 1,2,3 and 4

FOOTBALL SYSTEM

---

1 Enter information on all football players

2 Display table for all footballers

3 Update specific footballers goal tally

4 Exit from program

Select one of the above (1 to 4) **4**

Index